Path of Life

God Bless,

Chris

Path of Life

The Way of Wisdom for Christ Followers

G. Christopher Scruggs

20 April 2014

Easter Sunday

WIPF & STOCK · Eugene, Oregon

PATH OF LIFE
The Way of Wisdom for Christ Followers

Wipf & Stock
An Imprint of Wipf and Stock Publishers
199 W. 8th Ave., Suite 3
Eugene, OR 97401

www.wipfandstock.com

ISBN 13: 978-1-62564-437-4

Manufactured in the U.S.A.

All Scriptures not otherwise indicated are from the Holy Bible, New International Version. Copyright © 1973, 1978, 1984.

The illustrative vignettes contained in this book are all composites of many, many experiences of the author over many years of Christian service. No actual person, living or dead, is being described. Any similarity between a character in any vignette and any person living or dead is entirely coincidental.

Contents

Contents

Preface

This book began as a private study by a young lawyer. Later, it became a Bible study for a Sunday School class in Houston, Texas. More than twenty years have passed. The young lawyer is now a pastor just a few years away from retirement. Along the way, the little Bible study has been taught in a number of classes in Houston, in Richmond, Virginia, and in Brownsville and Memphis, Tennessee. Over the years, I have learned that there is no end to the search for wisdom. The wisdom we need for one stage of life is not the wisdom we need for another. I have also learned that one fails to take the advice of wisdom at one's own risk. If a person doesn't learn wisdom at the first opportunity, it will soon be too late, and damage will be done. Then, the first lesson and yet another will have to be learned!

In the day-to-day practice of ministry, I have the opportunity to work with people and their problems. The most common source of human problems is a lack of love and nurture at an early age. There is, however, a second source of human brokenness that is almost as serious—a lack of understanding concerning what it means to live wisely. Many people in our culture are making up their lives as they go along, without reference to the wisdom of the ages. The result is unnecessary failure, suffering, and loss. The student of wisdom literature receives all the benefits of studying any scripture: teaching for spiritual, moral, and practical maturity; rebuke for the ways in which we fall short; correction for our inadvertent mistakes; and a guide for training in righteousness (2 Tim 3:16–17). Wisdom literature does not solve all the problems of life. It does provide tools with which to address them.

My father loved proverbs and pithy sayings. I have joked many times about one particular saying: "If you want to dance, you have to pay the fiddler." Dad applied this proverb to an endless variety of situations: dating relationships, working hard, studying, managing money, and the like. I used to roll my eyes when he reminded me of that proverb—but, it has come to my aid more than once as an adult! I don't have my father's memory for short sayings like, "You can lead a horse to water, but you can't make him drink" (which meant not following his good advice). As a parent, I did not constantly repeat these proverbs to my children as my father did to me. Just occasionally I regret that I did not. My children lack many fond memories I possess.

As a pastor, I have come to believe that our society's propensity to devalue folk wisdom and the experiences of past generations deprives young people of an important kind of training—practical training in basic common sense and an orientation towards the world that is needed to successfully navigate life. This book, therefore, is a kind of sustained argument for the importance of valuing traditional wisdom and especially that wisdom that has its source in God.

Wisdom literature is less a detailed road map for life than a series of markers or road signs for the journey of life. Some years ago my wife and I spent time living and traveling in Scotland. During that trip we learned that when you don't know a country, you pay a lot more attention to road signs than you do when you are familiar with a place. One major problem of contemporary life is the assumption that we know where we are and how to get to where we are going. In school and early in our professional careers, we assume that if we stay with or just a bit ahead of our fellow travelers we are on the correct road. Only after a few wrong turns and minor and even major collisions do we conclude we need to find a road map and pay attention to the signs!

The first problem facing a serious student of wisdom literature is the sometimes disorganized diversity of wisdom teachings. Proverbs, for example, consists of a series of independent sayings often arranged in no easily discernible order. This makes a personal study difficult, particularly if the student is not (as I am not) gifted with a strong memory. To help solve this problem, I have written the first part of this book as a topical introduction to wisdom literature of the Old Testament from a Christian perspective.

A word about the notion of a "Christian perspective" on wisdom literature: the revelation of Jesus Messiah in the New Testament is the core element of a Christian perspective on Scripture. As the disciples reflected on the Cross, they came to the conclusion that the very being of God is love—a kind of self-giving love capable of endless sacrifice on behalf of the beloved (1 John 4:8). This understanding is central to the way in which Christians view the being of God, the teachings of Scripture, and the nature and purpose of wisdom literature. If a person reads wisdom literature from the perspective of a Christian, we meet One we did not expect to meet. I still remember how my heart leapt when I first read the words of Agur, Son of Jakeh, referred to as an Oracle:

> Who but God goes up to heaven and comes back down?
> Who holds the wind in his fists?
> Who wraps up the oceans in his cloak? Who has created
> the whole wide world? What is his name—and his son's
> name? Tell me if you know! (Prov 30:4 NLT)

In the words of the wise men and women of Israel, we unexpectedly come face to face with the Wisdom of God, and in coming into contact with the Wisdom of God, we come into contact with someone we may not have expected to meet—the One who was the Wisdom of God incarnate.

I hope all those who read this book will find a blessing in its pages.

Chris Scruggs
Memphis, Tennessee
Epiphany 2014

Acknowledgments

Years ago, I was privileged to teach with others a Sunday School class we called "The Carpenters Class." A study on Proverbs, from which this book evolved, was prepared for that class. The "Carpenters," all of whom our family remembers with love, allowed me to develop my gifts as a teacher, and they put up with my many failures. Thank you.

Since graduating from seminary, I have served two congregations, First Presbyterian Church, Brownsville, Tennessee, and Advent Presbyterian Church, Cordova, Tennessee. I have taught this study in one form or another in both of these churches and am grateful for that opportunity. Many folks at Advent proofed and made suggestions to the manuscript, and my special thanks are due to each and every one of them.

My wife Kathy Trammell Scruggs, to whom this book is dedicated, is the one person who needs to be thanked most of all. She helped proof the book, and in many ways, including allowing us to leave our home of many years, made this book possible.

To the many others who have given support, inspiration, love, and correction, I thank you.

Abbreviations

CEV   *Contemporary English Version*. New York: American Bible Society, 1995.

ESV   *English Standard Version*. Wheaton, IL: Crossway, 2005–2009.

Message   Peterson, Eugene H. *The Message: The Bible in Contemporary Language*. Colorado Springs: NavPress, 2003.

NCV   *New Century Version*. Dallas, TX: Word, 1991.

NIV   *The New International Version*. Colorado Springs: International Bible Society, 1984.

NKJV   *New King James Version*. Nashville, TN: Thomas Nelson, 1980.

NLT   *New Living Translation*. Wheaton, IL: Tyndale, 1996.

NRSV   *New Revised Standard Version Bible*. New York: Division of Christian Education of the National Council of Churches of Christ, 1989.

Phillips   Phillips, J. B. *The New Testament in Modern Language*. New York: Macmillan, 1958.

RSV   *Revised Standard Version*. New York: National Council of Churches, 1952.

Again, one preparing to sail and about to voyage over raging waves calls upon a piece of wood more fragile than the ship that carries him. For it was desire for gain that planned that vessel, and wisdom was the artisan who built it; but it is your providence, O Father, that steers its course, because you have given it a path in the sea, and a safe way through the waves, showing that you can save from every danger, so that even a person who lacks skill may put to sea.

THE WISDOM OF SOLOMON 14:1–4 (NRSV)

The Only Begotten and very wise Wisdom of God is the Creator and Framer of all things. . . . In order that what was made might not just be, but be "good" it pleased God that his own Wisdom should be implanted in Creation. Thus, God introduced and impressed his image on all in common and on each so that what was made might be the manifestly wise works and worthy of the Creator.

ST. ATHANASIUS ON PROVERBS 8

Books of Wisdom

Questions We Cannot Avoid

There are questions we cannot avoid in life. Everyone sooner or later must ask and answer questions such as: "What kind of life will bring me true happiness and fulfillment?" "How will I respond to failure?" "What kind of person should I marry?" "How shall I make a living?" "How will I respond to temptations?" "Which of the many opportunities of life will I take advantage of and which will I ignore?" "Why am I suffering?" "Why don't my achievements bring me happiness?" "What does the future hold?" We cannot ignore these and many other similarly important questions.

The wisdom tradition embodied in the Old Testament addresses all these questions and many more. My purpose is to work out the implications of Wisdom literature for the way in which Christians and others live in contemporary society. The wisdom tradition is one of three main traditions embodied in the Old Testament. Together with the Law and the Prophets, Wisdom literature exerts an important influence on the way in which Christians and Jews see and respond to the world. The God revealed in Jesus Christ is not only the All-Powerful and All-Loving God. The God of Israel revealed in Christ is also the All-Wise God in whom human beings find guidance for the mundane affairs of everyday life.

Jake graduated from high school nearly four years ago. He is the product of a broken home. After his father remarried, Jake seldom saw his father. He and his mother were close for a time after the divorce. He was her "little man." Eventually, she too remarried. Jake was never close to his stepfather, who seemed to favor his own children. In high school Jake was an underachiever. Talented and athletic, he never had the drive to excel at sports. Intelligent, but not gifted, he seldom studied and therefore made poor grades. He experimented with drugs. Lacking direction, he spent four years drifting from low paying job to low paying job, periodically living at home. Now twenty-two, he wonders if he can ever get his life on track. Jake recently turned to a pastor, a friend for many years who had been his youth leader. His pastor, who cares for Jake, spent a part of the day talking and sharing with Jake about life and about the challenges he faces. After Jake left, his pastor prayed for Jake and for the many young men and women just like him in the church, neighborhood, and city—children growing up without the benefit of the wisdom past generations took for granted, but which for the past sixty years or more has been discounted, ridiculed, and seldom taught to children as they grew up. The pastor wonders, "What is Jake to do? What am I to do about Jake and about the many young people just like him?"

Contemporary Christian thought often ignores the importance of wisdom in the conduct of our everyday lives and in our relationship with God. Although Christ is seen as the "Word of God," the eternal Logos or rationality of God in human form, and although Paul praises Christ as the "wisdom of God," the focus of Protestantism tends to be on the "hidden wisdom of the cross," on grace, faith, and salvation, as opposed to the practical implications of the incarnation for everyday life. This can leave people without the tools they need for successfully living out the life of faith.

Books of Wisdom

The wisdom tradition was an important part of the development of Jewish society. Wisdom literature is a valuable part of the cumulative reflection of the writers of Scripture on the experiences of Jewish history. Out of this reflection, they achieved a social order and a moral consensus concerning how people should live and arrange their lives.[1] Wisdom is found in every book of Holy Scripture. Certain books, however, have a special focus on wisdom and the questions wisdom raises. I have chosen to focus on five Old Testament books: Proverbs, Song of Songs, Job, Ecclesiastes, and Daniel.

Three of these wisdom books are written from the viewpoint of Solomon (the patron of wisdom): Proverbs, Ecclesiastes, and Song of Songs. Proverbs contains basic wisdom teaching. Ecclesiastes discusses the limitations of the search for wisdom in a way that is helpful to modern people. Song of Songs is a love poem. Job deals with a problem the wisdom school of Israel found difficult, if not impossible to resolve—the problem of undeserved suffering. The book is a sustained examination of the human experience of undeserved suffering and the loss of meaning it can entail.

I have treated Daniel as a wisdom book for a number of reasons. While Daniel is numbered among the Prophets in the Catholic and Protestant Bibles, it is contained among the Writings in the Jewish Bible. The book is best understood in the context of those writings in the Jewish Bible that are about how we live the life of faith in difficult times. Daniel was also remembered as a preeminent wise person in Old Testament literature. The stories of Daniel and of Joseph recorded in Genesis contain messages concerning the rewards of wisdom in public life amid the challenges of history.

Finally, Daniel and other eschatological books can be understood as examples of wisdom as it seeks understanding at the limits of human knowledge. Daniel is an apocalyptic book. In apocalyptic literature, the curtain of time, which forever hides the future from

1. Blenkinsopp, *Wisdom and Law*, 84.

our eyes, is partially ripped asunder, and we receive a glimpse into what humans have always wanted to know—the future. Our human desire to successfully meet the challenges of life drives us to understand where our personal history and the history of those we care for are leading. The eschatological passages in Daniel reflect this human desire to know how the story of our lives and of human history will end. This desire and the search of wisdom for the future terminate in the eschatological vision.

Scholars tell us that human beings think in terms of narrative—of stories.[2] We try to make sense of our lives in terms of a story, which story we hope will have a happy ending. Apocalyptic literature represents that moment in which God pierces the veil of the future and gives us a glimpse of the future of the human story. We see in narrative form the victory of the righteous, the defeat of evil, and the end of war and persecution for which all good people long. This glimpse of the future that Scripture gives enables Christians to follow the path that leads to divine life in the midst of a world characterized by suffering, sorrow, persecution, and defeat.

Wisdom and the Story of Our Lives

One reason for Christians to understand the perspective of the writers of wisdom literature is that our culture desperately needs to recover a sense that there is a moral order to the universe into which our life-stories fit. As a contemporary society we are often physically, morally, and spiritually rootless. Contemporary people have no coherent practical or moral grounding to face the problems and challenges of life. Rootlessness leads to a shallow life lived in a series of unconnected choices based on the impulses of the moment. Without a sustained vision of life, and without the wisdom of past generations, we are like all those who distain history: condemned to repeat the mistakes of the past and reap the consequences.

2. See, for example, Hauerwas and Jones, *Why Narrative?*

Cultural Location of Wisdom Literature

Scholars ask questions that bear upon authorship and also take the reader deeper into the question of the timing and reason for the wisdom literature. King Solomon's interest in proverbial wisdom is unquestionably one explanation for the origin of Proverbs, but there is more. David was the founder of a dynasty and an empire. He was a charismatic leader and warrior. His legitimacy was founded on his character and military leadership. Solomon, on the other hand, was a hereditary ruler. As such, he needed legitimacy and advisors, as would his successors. Solomon and his successors needed a bureaucracy to assist in ruling Israel. In the ancient world, rulers often sponsored schools that prepared young men to serve in the king's service. It is likely that wisdom literature had as one of its purposes educating leaders for Israel.

Parts of Proverbs and certain wisdom psalms show signs of having been created as teaching tools. The ancient world, Greek and Hebrew, was without the modern romantic notion that children raise themselves or that character is a simple product of the natural development of an inborn nature. For them, character was formed through education, example, and discipline. In fact, the most important part of education involved the creation of a certain kind of character.

One reason for the development of wisdom literature certainly involved training children and youth for public service, but the moral qualities that wisdom literature teaches go beyond the training of a few elites for service to royalty. Many proverbs are adapted to training any child. In fact, some psalms and proverbs show signs of being designed for the purpose of teaching good citizenship more than for transmitting principles of wise leadership. Therefore, it is not surprising that wisdom literature has always been seen as containing useful advice applicable to ordinary people as well as scholars.

The ancients understood that adults need instruction in wise living just as much as children. The inscription at the beginning of Proverbs is instructive:

> For learning about wisdom and instruction, for understanding words of insight, for gaining instruction in wise dealing, righteousness, justice, and equity, to teach shrewdness to the simple, knowledge and prudence to the young—let the wise also hear and gain in learning, and the discerning acquire skill to understand a proverb and a figure, the words of the wise and their riddles. (Prov 1:2–6 NRSV)

Everyone needs the lessons of wisdom, young and old, simple and smart.

In summary, Proverbs is the basic book of wisdom in the Old Testament. Ecclesiastes, Job, and Daniel represent the wisdom tradition as it struggles to understand particular problems: the problem of undeserved suffering (Job), the seeming meaninglessness of life (Ecclesiastes), maintaining faith in times of difficulty, and finding hope for the future (Daniel).

The Jewish Character of Biblical Wisdom Literature

Often readers of wisdom literature ignore its location in both Jewish and Christian Bibles. This habit results in over-emphasizing the differences between wisdom literature and other teachings of the Old and New Testaments. The authors and compilers of wisdom literature were Jews, familiar with the Law, the Prophets, and the Writings as they existed in their day and time. Jewish wisdom literature was collected, compiled, and read in the context of Jewish faith in the God of Abraham, Isaac, and Jacob who appeared to Moses in a burning bush and liberated them from bondage in Egypt. The early church, reflecting upon the revelation of Christ, incorporated Jewish understanding into the developing Christian notion of the meaning of Israel's history for the New Testament church.

The thematic inscription, "Deep respect for God is the beginning of knowledge" (Prov 1:7; author's paraphrase) alerts the reader that Proverbs is to be read in context as a part of Israel's faith in the One God revealed to Abraham and Sarah, Isaac and Rebekah, to the remaining patriarchs, to Moses at Mount Sinai, and to the disciples in Christ. Thus, wisdom literature is part of the gracious word of the God to those chosen to follow the Way of Life the Creator of the heavens and the earth imbedded into the nature of the universe and reveals by grace to the human race.

The compilers of the Old Testament viewed wisdom writings as a part of the revelation of the Lord God of Israel, now understood as the Triune One revealed in the life, death, and resurrection of Jesus, the Christ. The writers of the New Testament, steeped as they were in the history and tradition of Israel, understood and proclaimed that the One they worshiped as the crucified and risen Messiah was, at the same time, a revelation of the wisdom of God (1 Cor 1:30; Col 1:15–19). The early church identified the personification of wisdom found in Proverbs 8 with the word of God made flesh revealed in Jesus Christ.[3] The Wisdom of God appeared in Jesus of Nazareth as a full revelation of the true wisdom of God in human form.

Fundamental Teachings

As mentioned above, biblical wisdom literature is varied and complex. The wise men and women of Israel pondered many different aspects of human life—and they were not unaware of the limits of wisdom and paradoxes of human life. Nevertheless, as one studies these writers, certain themes emerge as foundational.

First, wisdom writers believed that, whatever foundation wisdom has in practical experience, the ability to usefully appropriate wisdom requires respect for God and for the wisdom through which the world was created (Prov 1:7; 9:10). Mere practical shrewdness is

---

3. See, for example, Athanasius, "Four Discourses Against the Arians," 357–93.

not sufficient for wise living. Wise living requires an awestruck, respectful, reverent relationship with God. This relationship produces humility, trust, and teachableness—prerequisites for the wise life.

Second, God created a world possessing a practical and moral order to which human beings must adapt if they are to live well. Examples of the practical order include the importance of working hard and the danger of debt or guaranteeing the debts of others. In the mind of the Jewish wise men, the wise person learns and adapts to this practical order God implanted in the world, whereas the fool ignores this order and suffers as a result. An example of the moral order is the sanctity of marriage and the dangers of adultery; moral understandings repeated over and over again in wisdom literature. The wise and righteous person learns and adapts to the moral order of God's creation. The fool and the wicked person violate this order and suffer as a result.

Third, central to attaining the blessings of the wise life is the intergenerational transmission of wisdom from parent to child. Parents have a duty to impart wisdom to their children, and children have a duty to listen to the advice and counsel of parents. The constant refrain, "Listen my child . . ." (Prov 4:1, 10; 5:1) bears witness to the importance of parental transmission of wisdom to their children. This transmission is not just oral, but also involves example and discipline.

Fourth, parental transmission is not the end of training for the wise life. Each individual has an obligation to continue to seek wisdom. Ultimately, children are responsible for their own future. It is not enough to listen while young and under parental authority. One must continue to seek wisdom throughout life. Learning the principles of wisdom and memorizing proverbs is no substitute for true character and wisdom written on the heart of each person.

Fifth, the order of society requires that people follow certain patterns and personal disciplines of life. When we have respect for the family, maintain sexual purity, honor friendships, maintain sobriety, work hard, save for financially difficult times, carry out shrewd business dealings, avoid excessive debt, uphold respect for government, and follow similar practices, we begin to form the contours of a wise and blessed life.

Sixth, business and politics are not exempt from the moral and spiritual order God embedded in the universe. Proverbs does not recognize a distinction between the morally proper action and the pragmatically useful action either in business or in government. The business leader and the political ruler are bound by the same moral rules as anyone else. In this particular observation, the worldview of the wise men and women of Israel differs most dramatically from the materialistic and pragmatic worldview of the Modern Age.

Finally, for the authors of wisdom literature, the good life is the blessed life. The writers of wisdom literature were not unaware of the moral quandaries facing one who attempts to live wisely. Particularly in Job, Ecclesiastes, and Daniel, wisdom writers explore the limits of our ability to understand God's order and issues of inexplicable suffering, failure, and the success and prosperity of the wicked. But, on the whole, they maintain that the moral life and blessed life are one and the same.

Conclusion

The journey from the cultural situation of the twenty-first century to the wisdom writers of ancient Israel brings us back to the present—to the problems and difficulties of our own age and culture. My hope is that an exploration of wisdom literature will help readers develop a kind of critical distance from our own culture and bring about receptivity to the voice of wisdom as we face the choices and challenges of everyday living.

We live at a juncture between the modern world, with its distrust of traditional wisdom and customs, and the emerging "postmodern" world, with its suspicion towards any truth claims at all. Both modernism and postmodernism are critical of religious claims to discern the purpose and meaning of creation and human history.

Postmodernism views such claims as mere bids for power, often implicitly endorsing a kind of pragmatic nihilism. The practical result of this perspective impacts anyone religious, political, or otherwise who makes a claim for the truthfulness of any proposition. This, in turn, has a profound, practical impact on the lives of people cut loose from traditions of faith and morals.

Against the most radical forms of postmodern thinking, this book suggests that wisdom literature embodies and summarizes a revelation founded in the religious and practical experience of generations. It involves passing down the practical conclusions of countless human beings concerning the nature of life and how to live wisely. The result is a body of literature full of what might be called "mental tools"—short, concise statements that focus on the kinds of challenges all human beings face.[4]

This product of generations of thinking and living is not the product of a single culture, but of a diverse group of cultures that span the period during which the biblical witness was recorded. The result involves sayings, stories, proverbs, parables, poetic teachings, and the like.[5] These literary forms direct our attention to moral and practical aspects of typical challenges of daily living in a variety of ways using a variety of literary devices. They are not substitutes for critical thinking in the midst of the problems of life. They are guides to our thinking about concrete problems.

Wisdom is a tool we use in day-to-day life. Tools require skill in use. Generally, the utility of a tool is only fully available to a craftsman trained and experienced in the proper use of the tool so that its use is second nature. Mental tools are no different. The value of wisdom literature is not in the study of it, or even in the memorization of its teachings, but in internalizing and consciously and unconsciously learning to live wisely over an extended period of time.

---

4. Polanyi, *Personal Knowledge*, 55–63. I use the term "mental tools" in the way suggested by Polanyi.

5. See von Rad, *Wisdom in Israel*, 24–50, for a full listing and scholarly analysis of the forms of wisdom in the Old Testament.

An example of this function of wisdom is the warnings of wisdom literature against laziness and against excessive work (cf. Prov 12:4 and 23:4). These proverbs provide a way of thinking about work and leisure. They are not a substitute for personal decision. They are an aid to thinking and acting, not a substitute for personal responsibility. This book intends to encourage readers to rediscover wisdom literature not as the solution to the problems of life but as a source of basic principles that we can apply in order to live wisely.

As we study, memorize, and meditate on wisdom literature, we learn to indwell its principles. Only when the principles of wisdom are internalized so they are tacitly available to us as part of our conscious and unconscious perception of the world can they perform their most important use in guiding thought and action.[6] This is why wisdom literature is important for young people to internalize at an early age, so that it can function to guide their perception and experience over the long course of their lives.

Modern Christian churches (including my own) have not done a sufficient job of providing members and children with the skills in living wisely required to meet the challenges of society and our prevailing culture. This book is designed to help Christians understand and respond to the challenges our culture presents to the wise life. I have attempted to connect wisdom literature with the greater narrative of Scripture to show how Old Testament wisdom fits into the greater story of God's wisdom and redeeming love.

---

6. Polanyi, *Tacit Dimension*. The work of Polanyi and its application to wisdom thinking is often noted during the course of this study.

Questions for Reflection

1. What kind of life will bring you true happiness and fulfillment?

2. How do you respond to failure?

3. Of the many opportunities of life, which ones should you take advantage of and which ones should you ignore?

4. Are you suffering in any way? Why?

5. Do your achievements bring you the happiness you thought they would?

6. What do you truly think the future holds for you?

Joyful is the person who finds wisdom,
 the one who gains understanding.
For wisdom is more profitable than silver,
 and her wages are better than gold.
Wisdom is more precious than rubies;
 nothing you desire can compare with her.
She offers you long life in her right hand,
 and riches and honor in her left.
She will guide you down delightful paths;
 all her ways are satisfying.
Wisdom is a tree of life to
 those who embrace her;
 happy are those who hold her tightly.

PROVERBS 3:13–18 (NLT)

1

What Is Wisdom?

I love to watch movies in which there are inscrutable Eastern wise men. When younger, I often watched the television series *Kung Fu*.[1] The show featured David Carradine playing the disciple of a blind Chinese kung fu expert. In the television show, each week Carradine traveled around the Old West as a fugitive from justice, solving some problem or righting some wrong. Of course, there was both a lot of esoteric wisdom and a lot of punching and kicking. This television program marked the beginning of popular America's fascination with Eastern religion and martial arts. In one of the most famous episodes, Master Po and Keith Carradine have the following exchange:

> Master Po: Close your eyes. What do you hear?
>
> Young Caine: I hear the water; I hear the birds.
>
> Po: Do you hear your own heartbeat?
>
> Caine: No.
>
> Po: Do you hear the grasshopper which is at your feet?
>
> Caine: Old man, how is it that you hear these things?
>
> Po: Young man, how is it that you do not?[2]

1. *Kung Fu*, ABC, 1972–1975.
2. "The Way of the Tiger, the Sign of the Dragon," season 1, episode 1, February 22, 1972.

This is the kind of esoteric, mystical, and difficult to understand wisdom the series popularized.

When the Bible speaks of "wisdom," is this what it is talking about? Certainly, there are parts of wisdom literature that seem esoteric and hard to understand, but that is not what the Old Testament normally means by "wisdom." There is nothing esoteric about the fundamental biblical idea of wisdom. In fact, most biblical wisdom literature is precisely the opposite: it is intensely practical, focused on the wisdom of this world.

What Is Wisdom?

Have you ever haggled over the price of an item in a market overseas or in Latin America? If you have, you understand how difficult a process it is—and how easy it is to be cheated! The word translated "wisdom" as used in Proverbs and other wisdom literature has as its root the kind of shrewdness a business person in an ancient Middle Eastern bazaar would need to conduct business. In this sense, wisdom includes the ability to size up people and situations and to respond to them appropriately and successfully. It is the ability to live life "profitably," that is, successfully meeting its challenges and getting the happiness, fulfillment, and joy we all desire. It is the ability to navigate the day-to-day details of earning a living, raising a family, providing for aging parents, raising children, and growing old. As such, wisdom is fundamentally a practical quality. The wise person has practical skills necessary to effectively face the problems of life. In other words a wise person has mastered the art of living well.[3]

To some degree, wisdom is the product of intelligence, insight, experience, and application; however, becoming wise is different than becoming smart or learning many different things. The wise person, whatever his or her Intelligence Quotient (IQ), must understand people and situations and have insight into their objectives and motivations. A wise person must be self-aware and think ahead, he

3. Unger and White, "Wisdom," 473.

or she must understand the consequences of words and deeds, and what others are likely to do in response to them. In this sense, wisdom involves foresight—the ability to think through a situation in such a way as to be able to understand the likely result of a course of action. There is nothing esoteric about that ability.

We have all known people who could answer abstract questions very easily and had a lot of information about a number of subjects, but who could not easily navigate the business of life. While it helps to be intelligent, wisdom is about more than intelligence. It is about the ability to put whatever intelligence God has given us to work effectively in the day-to-day task of living. One can be wise at every level or stage of human life, and one can also be foolish at that same level or stage of life. Although experience helps, as will be discussed below, age and experience is not enough. We have to learn from our experience. Most of us have heard a person described as having years of experience making the same mistakes over and over again. We can live life and grow in our ability to meet its challenges or we can simply make the same mistakes over and over again. The wise person learns from his or her mistakes and grows in wisdom, not making the same mistake over and over again.

Wisdom and Experience

The wise person will need more than the ability to simply foresee what may or may not occur in the future. The wise person will have the practical experience and understanding to devise an appropriate course of action in a given situation. Wisdom about practical matters requires experience. No one is born with the innate ability to sense the consequences of every possible course of action in every concrete situation. In addition, the more complicated the situation, the more experience is required to handle it! This runs against the grain of much popular thinking in our culture. For example, we tend to exalt the young person who makes a fortune, not the sixty-year-old who after decades of diligent service to a corporation or agency finally rises to a position of influence. While a young person may be wise and have the ability to succeed beyond his or her years, normally this is not the case.

Many years ago, in a different church from the one I now serve, there was a conflict—a destructive conflict that caused a church split. My wife and I were leaders in trying to hold the church together during that conflict. Years later, another congregation had to make a similar decision with all the potential for a similar conflict. Without the experience of almost twenty-five years earlier, I would not have been able to lead the congregation safely through that time. Experience is as important as ability when it comes to decision-making.

As a young lawyer, for a short time I tried lawsuits. Then I moved into the corporate and securities section of our firm. During a particular transaction, I was in the office of the partner in charge of the transaction, who also had a background in litigation. I mentioned that I did not feel good about a certain course of action but could not put my finger on what was wrong. He looked over his desk and said, "That is the litigator's sick stomach." He meant that experience in lawsuits makes one sensitive to the dangers of litigation—and creates an instinct concerning when litigation is about to result from a course of action.

One value of experience is that it makes a person cautious in situations that may involve physical, moral, spiritual, financial, or other danger. People can be wise only within the limits of their experience and ability to respond to problems. Unfortunately, young people have seldom lived long enough, experienced enough problems, and failed and picked themselves up enough to be wise with respect to all the many, many problems life brings. Although age is important, it is the experience and skill that experience brings that is crucial. Almost no one can be wise in any area of life without some degree of experience in it.

Wisdom and Insight

Biblical wisdom involves a quality the Bible calls "insight." Just as the word indicates, insight is the capacity to "see into" a person or situation. John tells a story from early in Jesus' ministry. When the time came for Passover, Jesus went to Jerusalem. There he saw the moneychangers in the temple and observed the corruption of the temple system. He took cords, made a whip, and drove out moneychangers. When he was confronted with a demand for a miracle, he responded, "Destroy this temple and I will raise it again in three days" (John 2:19). He was referring to his death and resurrection, but people took him literally and could not understand him. As a result of his teaching many people believed in him but for the wrong reason. The story ends with this observation: "But Jesus didn't trust them, because he knew human nature. No one needed to tell him what mankind is really like" (John 2:24–25 NLT). Jesus "saw" into situations and people. Insight involves the ability to "see into" a person, group of persons, or a situation and respond wisely to it.

Wisdom and Understanding

With insight comes another quality that wise people must have—understanding. No one can possibly respond wisely to a situation without understanding it. The term "understanding" literally means to "stand under." To have understanding means to know what is under the surface of things. To understand persons or situations is to have some idea what motivates people and what forces are at work in a given situation. It means looking beneath the surface of things to perceive motivations and forces not easily discerned. Understanding involves familiarity with people and circumstances such that one can foresee what people will do and where a course of action will lead.

Much biblical wisdom literature involves gaining the kind of insight that leads to understanding. For example, early in Proverbs the young person is warned to avoid violence. After a graphic description of the character of a group of violent highway robbers, Proverbs says, "These men lie in wait for their own blood, they ambush only themselves" (Prov 1:16). The Bible is encouraging young people to avoid a life of crime and violence and to understand its consequences. Hopefully when we see how a violent life will end, we have enough insight to avoid it.

In 1967, the movie *Bonnie and Clyde* was released. The movie glorified the careers of Bonnie Parker and Clyde Barrow, bank robbers who terrorized Texas and parts of the Midwest during the 1930s.[4] They had a hideout in Joplin, Missouri, near our family's home in Springfield, Missouri. Clyde Barrow was a sociopath and a murderer. Eventually, law enforcement officers, led by famous Texas Ranger Frank Hamer, ambushed and killed both of them. Bonnie Parker was twenty-four when she died; Clyde Barrow was twenty-five. To young moviegoers, the wild life of Bonnie and Clyde seemed exciting. The truth is they lived short, violent, unhappy, unhealthy, unbalanced, and ultimately futile lives. In the end, they were ambushed and killed. In truth they ambushed themselves by the way they lived.

The wise person has the kind of understanding that Bonnie and Clyde lacked. Instead of being attracted to easy money, loose living, violence, and death, the wise person understands that happiness comes with hard work, faithful relationships, and peacefulness—virtues wisdom literature promotes. Understanding is the capacity to "see in our minds" the consequences of a course of action or style of life and make good choices.

David is a rebel. For whatever reason, in his younger years, he never quite fit in. His family moved a good deal, and his father drank heavily. Eventually, he left David's mother. David almost never saw his father during his early adolescence. David's mother, never particularly strong, allowed him a lot of freedom and rarely disciplined him for wild behavior.

---

4. *Bonnie and Clyde*, Warner Brothers, 1967.

Not a good student or athletic, David fell in with a group at his school involved in drugs. Naturally, his grades suffered. Eventually, David began selling drugs and engaging in small time criminal activity associated with dealing illegal substances. Two weeks ago, he was present when something went wrong with a drug deal and shots were fired, injuring a young person. David was identified and arrested. He is now in jail waiting for his mother to raise the bail necessary for his release. He never saw this coming.

Self-Discipline and Prudence

Of course, no one gains wisdom and insight without discipline, self-discipline, and habits of prudence in thought and behavior. Proverbs begins by giving the purpose of wisdom and the reason the collectors of the book put it together: "Their purpose is to teach people wisdom and discipline, to help them understand the insights of the wise. Their purpose is to teach people to live disciplined and successful lives, to help them do what is right, just, and fair. These proverbs will give insight to the simple, knowledge and discernment to the young" (Prov 1:2–4 NLT). The purpose of wisdom is to create people with the kind of self-discipline and practical wisdom to react to life wisely.

Living wisely involves more than understanding. It involves action. Wise living can only be achieved by those who have the willpower to discipline themselves not to act on impulse, but to think through the consequences of a course of action, to avoid chasing temporary and ultimately unimportant pleasures, and to treat others fairly. Wise living requires the discipline to constantly put into practice the teachings of wise mentors. None of this comes natural to human beings. It requires discipline when we are young and self-discipline when we reach adulthood.

Wisdom for Life

As mentioned at the beginning of this chapter, when many contemporary people hear the word, "wisdom" they too often think of some kind of esoteric knowledge unrelated to practical life. Sometimes we think of wisdom in connection with "philosophy," which means "the love of wisdom," as interesting only to a few academics. This is not the way wisdom literature should be understood. Wisdom is the kind of knowledge that permits effective thought and action. Wisdom is never merely abstract knowing. It is a kind of personal knowledge and experience that leads to—and is revealed in—action. This is why we speak of one person as a "wise investor," of another as a "wise teacher," of still another as a "wise counselor," and on and on. Wisdom is a form of practical reasoning. Wisdom is where knowledge and experience meet in prudent action.

The Value of Wisdom

At one point in Proverbs, the writer says, "Wisdom is supreme; therefore get wisdom. Though it cost all you have, get understanding" (Prov 4:7). In the prior chapter the value of wisdom is compared to fine jewels and precious metals:

> Blessed are those who find wisdom, those who gain understanding, for she is more profitable than silver and yields better returns than gold. She is more precious than rubies; nothing you desire can compare with her. (3:13–15)

Those who gain wisdom, insight, understanding, discipline, and prudence gain the most important thing in the entire world.

There is no area of life that wisdom does not enrich. Personally, it is the secret of having the kind of character that can face the challenges of life. In the family, it is the secret of a strong, faithful marriage and of raising children prepared for life. Economically, it is the secret of having enough and of avoiding seeking to have too much. Politically, it is the secret of a stable and prosperous nation.

The wisdom human beings most need is that which enables us to live successful, happy, fulfilled lives. This is why wisdom is called a "Path of Life" or a "Tree of Life." The result of wisdom is a full, complete, joyful, prosperous, and happy life so far as human thinking and acting can create one.

Questions for Reflection

1. When you think of "wisdom," what do you normally think of? After reading this chapter, what is your definition of wisdom?

2. Do you think you have the ability to see into people and situations and understand their objectives and motivations? If so, why do you think so?

3. Do you regard yourself as a self-disciplined person or as a person lacking in discipline? In what areas of your life would you like to increase self-discipline?

4. In what area of life would you like to have more wisdom? What kind of experiences do you think you need to become wiser?

These sayings bear the name of the wisest king of God's People, the son of their greatest king. These sayings allow God's people to become wise, be insightful, develop a disciplined and prudent life, and do what is appropriate for everyone. The wisdom this book teaches gives prudence to simple folks, and knowledge and discretion to young people. Even wise persons benefit from listening to these words of wisdom, becoming even wiser. Those who study wisdom add to their understanding, receiving guidance needed for living successfully.

PROVERBS 1:1–5 (AUTHOR'S PARAPHRASE)

2

The Source and Use of Wisdom

Where Do We Go for Wisdom?

We live in a world awash in information. In seconds, we can connect to the internet, ask a question, and find hundreds or thousands of responses. Major cities have vast libraries full of books about any possible question we might have. Can we trust the answers? Each week in writing sermons, I look up questions on the internet. A lot of the time, the answers given are overly simplistic or even dead wrong. As a voracious reader, I've read a lot of books only to conclude the author was wrong or misleading in his or her conclusions. Just having access to information does not mean that the information we get will be accurate or help us to live wisely.

In our culture, most young people begin looking to their peers for answers to important life questions in their teen years. Much of the time, the answers they receive reflect the understanding of a young person—and sometimes the understanding of a troubled young person. Should we just trust the opinions of our friends? Even when we are older, we often rely on the advice of people who share our interests, our profession, our hobbies, or our social situation in seeking to answer important questions of life. Is this enough?

The modern era has produced a great skepticism about traditional wisdom. A major question in the modern and postmodern world concerns questions like, "Can we trust those who came before us?" or "Is there a reliable way for us to know how to behave when the past seems so distant and backward in so many ways?" Much of the time popular authors answer the question, "Can we trust those who came before us?" with a resounding, "No." This is often very unfortunate and can lead people to make very poor choices. Although we need to question tradition, we also need to respect the wisdom of those who came before us.

The Human Authors of Proverbs

The collectors of the book of Proverbs inscribed Solomon's name at the beginning of the book—Solomon, the wisest king of Israel, the son of King David, the greatest of her kings (Prov 1:1). By tradition, Solomon loved wisdom and governed Israel wisely during the early years of his reign. As a leader, Solomon was a practical person, a king, a capable manager, and a shrewd businessperson. He was by reputation the wealthiest person in Israel's history. This inscription, which we often overlook, is saying to us, "If you want to know how to succeed in life, this is a book you must read. Someone who demonstrated exceptional wisdom wrote it. You can trust the wisdom of this book."

Solomon was not only personally wise; he was the patron of a group of wise men and women. In the ancient world, just as today, political leaders needed advisors. One reason for the development of wisdom literature was to provide instructional materials to produce wise administrators and counselors. In order to produce these administrators and counselors, kings supported schools of wisdom. These schools were designed to produce leaders for the nation.

Daniel is an example of a naturally, even supernaturally, wise young man. He was also the product of a program deliberately established by King Nebuchadnezzar to develop people who could assist in the leadership of the Neo-Babylonian Empire. Daniel begins with the story of his training for work in the court of Nebuchadnezzar:

> Then the king ordered Ashpenaz, chief of his court offi-
> cials, to bring in some of the Israelites from the royal family
> and the nobility—young men without any physical defect,
> handsome, showing aptitude for every kind of learning,
> well informed, quick to understand, and qualified to serve
> in the king's palace. (Dan 1:3–4a)

Daniel was chosen to be trained to be part of the bureaucracy and leadership of Nebuchadnezzar's empire. He was selected because of his natural talents that could be developed by a special kind of education. This special education developed his natural capacities for wise discernment and prudent decision-making.

The importance of wisdom literature, and especially proverbs, in assisting the rulers of the ancient world is supported by Proverbs 25:1, which speaks of proverbs of King Solomon being collected by the scribes of King Hezekiah, who ruled approximately two hundred years after Solomon died.[1] The book mentions two other royal authors, Augur, son of Jakeh of Massa (30:1) and Lemuel, king of Massa (31:1). Therefore, one can easily see that it is very likely that at least some of Proverbs was collected as part of the training of counselors for the kings and leaders of Israel.

A portion of Proverbs (22:17—24:22) draws on an Egyptian work, the *Instruction of Amenemopet* (1000–600 BC).[2] This indicates that wisdom literature of Israel was part of a larger wisdom movement, a movement that included Israel, as well as some of its surrounding neighbors. Perhaps Solomon himself began the process of collecting the wisdom of Israel and its neighbors and molding that collection into a training manual. Yet, this training manual did not simply copy the wisdom of other peoples—it was edited and revised

---

1. Solomon reigned from approximately 971 to 931 BC. Hezekiah reigned from about 729 to about 700 BC, or about two hundred years after Solomon.

2. Aiken, "Proverbs," 3.

in light of the faith of God's people in the God of Israel, the God of Abraham, Isaac, and Jacob.

The Divine Author of Wisdom

Whenever one speaks of the human source of a book in the Bible, there is a chance that people will mistake recognizing the importance of human sources for a denial of divine revelation. Wisdom literature seems so practical that it is easy to ignore its revelatory aspect. Human authors and editors, belonging to many different cultures and time periods, reflect the intricate way in which God used wise men and women and their literary skills to produce a series of books that are a "tree of life" to those who read them. The human authors did their part, but it is God who oversaw the creation of wisdom literature, for it is the wisdom of God of which the books speak. On one hand, wisdom literature is the product of human reflection. On the other hand, words near the beginning of Proverbs alert the reader to another, deeper level at which wisdom literature is read by Christians and Jews. "For the Lord gives wisdom, and from his mouth come knowledge and understanding" (2:6). The insight that God is the ultimate source of wisdom is fundamental to the wisdom tradition.[3]

The writers of wisdom literature saw in the practical experience of everyday life evidence of the work of God having religious and moral significance. In writing down human words, the writers believed they were also recording the word of God speaking through the events of everyday life. The written wisdom of the writers points toward and reveals the will of the One who created the world and who embedded meaning, value, and purpose into that creation (Prov 8:22–31; Ps 19). In the words of the writer of Second Peter,

---

3. See also Psalm 111:10: "Fear of the Lord is the foundation of true wisdom. All who obey his commandments will grow in wisdom. Praise him forever!" (NLT) and Proverbs 9:10: "The fear of the Lord is the beginning of wisdom, and the knowledge of the Holy One is insight" (ESV).

the authors were "carried along by the spirit" as they undertook their work (2 Pet 1:21).

This conviction that the human words of Scripture contain and point to the divine word of God finds expression in the New Testament where Holy Scripture is described as "God breathed" (2 Tim 3:16). This God-breathed divine word is "useful for teaching, rebuking, correcting, and training in righteousness so that the person of God is thoroughly equipped for every good work" (vv. 16–17). It is in this way that wisdom literature should be read—as a revelation given to the human race of the way in which human beings ought to think and live.

In wisdom literature God alerts a reader to the personal character of wisdom teaching. In Proverbs 8, wisdom is personalized as present with God in creation (vv. 22–27). Earlier in the chapter, wisdom personified "calls out" to the human race (v. 1). Over and over again, wisdom is described as in some way personal. In the New Testament, the Eternal Word of God, the second person of the Trinity, is described as coming and dwelling among the human race in the person of Christ—a personal appearance of the Divine Wisdom of God (see John 1:1–13). These and other passages point to the personal character of wisdom. Wisdom is a personal communication from a personal God to the human race.

The notion that God is speaking to us in and through personal communication is central to Christian faith. Christians believe that God is love. When we read Scripture faithfully, and pray to God earnestly, when we are aware of God in our day-to-day lives, the Divine Lover can be trusted to communicate with us. Like any recipient of a truthful communication made in love, we must listen with personal commitment and attentiveness. God is a God of mercy and of grace. Grace is essentially a form of self-giving, self-disclosure by an all-loving God. In and through the words of the wisdom writers, God speaks, giving guidance for specific circumstances of life. Too often we fail to read the Bible expecting to encounter a divine word applicable to the problems of everyday life. If we read wisdom literature in this way, we may be surprised at the result.

Thomas is sitting in a waiting room about to be admitted to his third drug treatment program. His mother nervously sits beside him. His father had a business meeting out of town that he did not want to cancel. Thomas grew up in an upper-middle-class family. He went to a private school, where he did well for his first several years. Then, he began drinking and taking illicit recreational drugs. From that time forward, his life has been one of increasing frustration and failure. At twenty-six his parents have watched him fail over and over again. He has been chronically unemployed since he left college. He has bounced from job to job, never really fitting in wherever he worked. In most cases, he was a model employee for a short while, but after a time his poor work ethic combined with a lack of anger control resulted in termination. As Thomas's mother sits nervously by her son, she is filled with guilt and shame. In her mind, she and her husband are responsible for the problems Thomas and their other children have experienced—drug addiction, divorce, and marital infidelity. She is wondering what they did wrong, and she does not know where to turn for help.

Many years ago, I was in a difficult business situation—and it was not getting better. For many months, wisdom teachings that warn about debt and guaranteeing the debts of others came to my attention. Eventually, these warnings dominated my thinking about the problem. I decided to take an unpopular action and refuse to go further, eliminating my guarantee in connection with an investment. It turned out that this was a good decision. Over months and months, God spoke in and through the words of the Bible to answer my need in very specific ways. The words of Scripture did not eliminate a need for personal participation and decision. They did not provide a rule I could blindly follow. Instead these words provided a mental peg upon which I could dwell in making my own decision. The communication of Scripture was like the advice of a good friend—a personal suggestion spoken in friendship, but the decision was still mine.

The Kind of Wisdom Found in Proverbs

The purpose of proverbial wisdom is to form hearts and minds so that human beings may know how to live wisely (Prov 1:2). Proverbs begins by stating its purpose: that all kinds of people may come to understand principles of successful and moral living (v. 3). Wisdom literature, therefore, developed as a way of expressing a practical understanding of how we are to live well and face the problems and possibilities of life successfully.

A root meaning of the Hebrew word for wisdom connotes the kind of shrewdness one expects of a successful trader in a Middle Eastern bazaar. Therefore, the first important purpose of reading wisdom literature is to develop patterns of thinking and insight that enable one to navigate life and its problems successfully. Over and over, wisdom literature emphasizes that a wise person does not believe all that he or she sees. First impressions are dangerous. Emotions need to be disciplined. Desires need to be resisted. These notions must not simply be in our minds. Instead, our hearts, our character must be formed wisely so that our instincts are to act in ways that are wise and productive.

I have a friend and prayer partner who, for many years, led a difficult life. He made many mistakes and suffered as a result. None of this involves particularly happy memories. This person is, however, one of the shrewdest judges of character I know. It is very, very hard to deceive my friend or to pull the wool over his eyes. He has developed a deep wisdom and insight concerning people and situations.

The wise person learns not to be satisfied with the surface of things but to develop insight into the reality of situations and into the motivations of people. Such a person is characterized by self-discipline and caution. Self-discipline involves resisting physical, emotional, and mental impulses. Caution requires thinking carefully about the downside of possible courses of action.

Young people, because they lack experience, particularly need to learn wisdom and restraint (v. 4). The worst mistakes we can make—mistakes that can warp and deform our future—are avoided by developing good judgment and caution when we are young. Therefore, young people especially need to develop the kind of character that understands the importance of instruction and moral reasoning. When they do they will learn to act in ways that are appropriate and fair to others. To do so, they need wise instruction and wise examples.

The journey of wisdom is not over when a person has achieved adulthood. Adults who have achieved a measure of wisdom still must pay attention to the teachings of wisdom. By doing this they add to their wisdom, deepen their understanding of life's mysteries, and understand more deeply how to meet life's challenges. This is so because every stage of life and every circumstance of life require different actions in different situations. Finally, all people need continual training in wisdom during the course of their lives—even those the world considers wise—or they will descend into foolishness (Rom 1:21–22).

In the modern world, and perhaps even more deeply in the emerging postmodern world, we have lost this understanding that we stand on the shoulders of those who have gone before us and who have faced the challenges of life. If we do not learn from their experience, we are doomed to repeat their worst mistakes. Too often in our culture, young people and their teachers lack respect for the past and for the lessons parents and others have learned. One of the saddest experiences of a pastor is when we are confronted with a young person who is deliberately refusing to learn a lesson of wisdom from a parent or other adult. Often the parent or adult has suffered as a result of some piece of foolishness and warns a child against it, only to be ignored. One very good example has to do with alcohol and drugs. More than once a parent with an addictive past has warned a child about the potential consequences of using drugs and been ignored, and with terrible consequences.

More deeply, many in our contemporary society have lost confidence that the world is an orderly creation of a wise and loving

God. This God has spoken to us in creation and through the writers of Holy Scripture. He even revealed himself to us personally in Jesus Christ, so that we can see what a fully loving and fully wise life looks like. Therefore, one of the most important tasks of our day is to recover an understanding that the world has a physical, spiritual, and moral order—an order we foolishly defy at our own risk. Many people have a sense that the modern and emerging postmodern world have created societies that are shallow and in constant danger of damaging people and the hopes and dreams of future generations. In order to give hope to future generations, we must recover the deposit of wisdom left to us by past generations.

Questions for Reflection

1. Who are the three persons indicated to be compilers or authors of portions of Proverbs?

2. What distinguished Solomon as a king? (1 Kings 3:4–12; 2 Chronicles 1:7–12)

3. Beyond the human author, who did the Jews believe to be the author of the Wisdom?

4. When you think of the word "wisdom," what do you think of? Do you connect wisdom with practical understanding? If so, how?

The fear of the Lord is the beginning of wisdom,
and knowledge of the Holy One is Insight.

Proverbs 9:10 (RSV)

Trust in the Lord with all your heart and lean not on your own understanding; in all your ways acknowledge him, and he will make your paths straight. Do not be wise in your own eyes; fear the Lord and shun evil. This will bring health to your body and nourishment to your bones.

Proverbs 3:5–8

3

The Heart Attitude of the Wise

Most of us remember a time when we felt that our parents, pastors, and teachers were hopelessly behind the times. One of our children at the ripe old age of fourteen announced to us: "Your job is done. I am raised now. I can take care of myself." Many of us never announced that to our parents, but we had the same adolescent, prideful idea that we had reached the point where we knew pretty much all that our parents and elders had to teach us. Most human beings reach a point sometime in life where we temporarily lose the habit of trusting God for the answers to life's questions—and a number of us never developed the habit.

Jeremy is twenty-nine and just entering his seventh year of full-time employment. Jeremy has had several jobs, none of which he kept for an extended period of time. In the end, he has always had conflict with his supervisors and fellow employees, who describe him as "arrogant." Jeremy is a committed Christian and always attempted to bring his faith to bear on decisions at work. In fact, most of his fellow employees admired his values and dedication. Recently, Jeremy went in to see a counselor about his work issues. It was not long before the counselor identified arrogance as a problem. Jeremy has been working on changing the way he interacts with others. Interestingly, Jeremy has noticed that he feels better about his work relationships and about the quality of his decisions. "As I have worked on not seeming to be a know-it-all, I have come to see that I really don't know it all. I am beginning to understand how limited my understanding of people and situations really is. It has even affected my faith. Now I sense in my heart what it means to have a deep humility born of an understanding of how little anyone really knows—especially about other people."

The Awesome Respect God Deserves

Most versions translate the motto of Proverbs as, "The *fear* of the Lord is the beginning of wisdom" (1:7; emphasis added). Right away, those with only a contemporary perspective have a problem with this statement. The idea that we should be motivated by "fear" is not congenial to our way of thinking. We have the notion that a person ought to be motivated by love or admiration. It is, therefore, important for people with this mindset to understand why and in what sense wisdom writers spoke as they did and the nature of the "fear" we ought to have for God.

In the ancient world, rulers were to be feared and respected. God, as the ultimate and supreme ruler of the universe, was to be feared and respected above all persons and powers (Col 6:10–12). To the ancient Jews, the Lord God of Israel was not just another god among many. The God of Israel was the supreme creator and ruler of all. The Lord God Almighty was not just a god, but the only, all powerful God. Jehovah God was not just a powerful force in the world but the most powerful and important force in the world. God was to be feared and respected, and worshiped above anything or anyone else.

In the modern, democratic West, people do not think "fear" to be an appropriate word to describe the relationship of citizens towards their rulers or government. This is one reason why, in the paraphrase of Proverbs 1:7 at the beginning of this chapter, I substituted the word "respect." Unfortunately, the word "respect" does not fully describe the quality of our relationship with God, even for modern people. There is more than simply "respecting" God for his status as the Creator of the world. We respect the president for his status as leader of our country. Elections, however, give citizens some degree of control over elected leaders. God, on the other hand, remains the uncontrollable source of all that is and will ever be, immeasurably beyond our control or direction. Therefore, the respect we must have for God is infinitely greater than the respect we have for people, however important.

The respect we must have for God is a deep respect for someone infinitely wiser and more powerful than ourselves. When I was young, just once, I put my finger in a wall electric outlet. After that experience, I learned to respect the power of electricity. To tell the truth, I am a bit afraid of electricity to this day. When I have to perform some home repair involving electricity, I am extremely careful. I don't want to end up shocked ever again. Friends who have attended launches of the space shuttle tell of the tremendous power required for a launch. Even miles away, the lift-off shakes the ground. The power that launches a space shuttle has the force of many bombs. Uncontrolled, it could cause great damage. That kind of power needs to be respected.

Years ago, while working on a "tie gang" near Black Rock, Arkansas, I looked up and saw a freight train bearing down upon our small group of workers. Because of unusual circumstances, our foreman had not given the normal warning to get off the tracks. Faced with the oncoming power of that locomotive, all members of that tie gang finished what we were doing and ran to get safely off those tracks. The sheer speed, energy, and power of the train compelled us to work better and faster than we would normally have been able to work. We respected the power of that train. In a similar way, we should respect the silent, patient, loving, but uncompromising power of God.

The path of wisdom begins with respecting the One who is the ultimate power behind all the powers in and of the created universe. Christians confess that we believe in "God the Father Almighty, the Creator of the Heavens and the Earth." The word "Almighty" clues us into the fact that, when we deal with God, we are dealing with One who is the ultimate source of power, including the power of wise living. Thus, the source and ground of all human wisdom lies beyond human wisdom—even beyond created reality. It is a power we cannot control. We can only respect it and live in awareness of its reality. The source and ground of wisdom is the "Deep Light" of the uncreated wisdom of an all-wise, all-loving, and all-powerful God.

The Nicene Creed, the one universal statement of faith of the Christian Church reads, "We believe in one God the Father Almighty, Maker of heaven and earth, *and of all things visible and invisible.*"[1] The addition of "all things visible and invisible" is important because it reminds us that God is the author both of things we do see, like a chair, and things that we don't see, like mathematics, the equations that govern the universe, the moral law, truth, beauty, and goodness. In God the physical world and the mental and moral world have their source, and he is the Lord over all things, what we see and what we do not see. Such a God deserves our deepest honor and respect.

Once we have a proper respect for God, something wonderful happens: we have a sense of our own limited understanding and power. We become humble and, in humility, we become teachable. This attitude is important in any kind of learning. To learn, we must have respect for our teachers, for those who went before us in the area we are studying, for the subject matter we are studying, and for the reality it is intended to illuminate. To learn anything, we must understand that we do not know everything we need to know. Without a humble respect for teachers, for a tradition, and for a reality outside us, it is impossible to learn anything.

---

1. Nicene Creed, 1.1; emphasis added. The Nicene Creed (AD 325) is the only creed used by all churches. It teaches that God is the Creator and lord not just of what we do see, but also of all we do not see (i.e., the spiritual and noetic worlds).

Wisdom literature teaches that the "Fear of the Lord is instruction in wisdom; and humility comes before honor" (Prov 15:33 ESV). These two great qualities, respect for God and a sense of personal humility, are deeply related to one another and necessary for the wise life. Without a sense of our own finite, limited understanding, we cannot have the kind of humility that believes, hopes, and loves under the guidance of a loving God. Without a sense of the infinite wisdom and power of God, we will not trust and properly respect the source of wise living.

Respecting the Divine Lover

This brings us to a specifically Christian understanding of what is meant by respecting and revering God. In the First Letter of John, we read:

> God is love, and whoever abides in love abides in God, and God abides in him. By this is love perfected with us, so that we may have confidence for the day of judgment, because as he is so also are we in this world. There is no fear in love, but perfect love casts out fear. For fear has to do with punishment, and whoever fears has not been perfected in love. (1 John 4:16–18 ESV)

A Christian fear of God is a loving response of deep, humble respect towards the One who first loved us, who draws us into his community of love, who gave himself for us, and who now dwells within in love.

God is not a cosmic despot. God is the divine father who loves us enough to take on our humanity, suffer our human limitations, and die for our pervasive foolishness, error, and sin in order to heal our separation from the source of divine wisdom. Our relationship with God should not be characterized by fearful obedience, but by a loving response to God's self-giving love. Thus, the "fear" of which wisdom literature speaks is actually a loving, reverent, respectful response to our divine parent who loves us and wishes us the best in life.

The wisdom imparted by God the Father is the source of both a natural and supernatural kind of living. It is *natural* in that it connects us with the world as God created it and human beings as they are. It is *supernatural* in that it is not finally grounded in the created order or in our own wisdom or experience. The wisdom of which the Bible speaks is the wisdom of the Creator God, the ground and source of all human existence and of everything that is or will be, and of whatever character it may have.

This is why "the fear of the Lord" is the beginning of wisdom. Without respect for God and trust in his faithful and orderly creation of the world and of human life, we have not taken the first step—a step that puts us into a proper relationship with the personal God who created and sustains all things by his wisdom, love, and power and who loves his creation, including the human race in general and us in particular. Once we have deep respect for God, we develop an appropriate self-confidence based upon a relationship with God. This relationship with God is a fountain of life and a source of wisdom for our lives (Prov 14:26–27). The wise person humbly seeks a godly wisdom that is "pure, then peace-loving, considerate, submissive, full of mercy and good fruit, impartial and sincere" (Jas 3:17). Such a person reacts wisely and without pride to the problems of life. Developing awe and respect for God does not result in fearful, dependent lives. A life-giving relationship with God and others results in humble self-confidence. This kind of wisdom can only be gained in a personal relationship with the One who is the source of all wisdom.

The Unimaginable Wisdom God Reveals

This reverent respect for God, the One Who Is and Will Be, is the beginning place of our search for wisdom. Christians do not believe that we can be content with simple worldly shrewdness in order to live wisely and well. The deepest wisdom, what I have elsewhere called "Deep Light," is the uncreated wisdom of God.[2] This wisdom is reflected in the material order of the universe and in the moral order of the world we human beings inhabit. However, as wonderful as practical and scientific understanding may be, as magnificent as the meditations of the great moral thinkers of the past may be, they point toward One who is the inexhaustible source and ground of wisdom and understanding. God's wisdom is the deepest wisdom of all.

We cannot come to the end of God's infinite wisdom. Throughout the Old Testament, God teaches his people that his wisdom is ultimately beyond human understanding. By the time of Isaiah, the prophets understood that the full nature of divine wisdom was beyond human understanding. God speaks through Isaiah saying,

> "For my thoughts are not your thoughts, neither are your ways my ways," declares the Lord. "As the heavens are higher than the earth, so are my ways higher than your ways and my thoughts than your thoughts." (Isa 55:8–9)

It was the conviction of the Jews that, while human wisdom reflects God's wisdom, God's wisdom infinitely transcends human wisdom. The rationality of the universe and its moral and aesthetic character reflect and point to a greater wisdom by which and through which the world was created.

The secret wisdom of God reveled in Christ is immeasurably greater than any human wisdom. Paul, when he writes of the revelation of Christ to the early church, puts it this way:

> Where is the one who is wise? Where is the scribe? Where is the debater of this age? Has not God made foolish the wisdom of the world? For since, in the wisdom of God, the world did not know God through wisdom, God decided, through the foolishness of our proclamation, to save those who believe. For Jews demand signs and Greeks desire

2. Scruggs, *Centered Living*. The term "the One Who Is and Will Be" is the way that book refers to the God of Israel.

wisdom, but we proclaim Christ crucified, a stumbling-block to Jews and foolishness to Gentiles, but to those who are the called, both Jews and Greeks, Christ the power of God and the wisdom of God. For God's foolishness is wiser than human wisdom, and God's weakness is stronger than human strength. (1 Cor 1:20–25 NRSV)

Paul perceived that in Christ the God of Israel revealed a surprising hidden wisdom that forms the basis of God's being, love, and power. This power is a wise love that works in self-giving sacrifice and weakness, even to the point of dying on a cross. This is a "secret" or hidden wisdom that humans can only receive by revelation. After all, who would expect that the heart of the all-powerful God of Abraham, Isaac, and Jacob is unlimited, self-giving, self-sacrificial love? Without the cross no one would ever have guessed at the full and deepest nature of God's wisdom.

The Wisdom of Common Grace Revealed to Faith

Despite the limits of human wisdom, human reflection on life and its problems reveals an orderly universe and a common human situation to which men and women may conform as they live and work in the everyday world. This human aspect of wisdom is not to be despised or undervalued. In fact, human understanding and wisdom are the most valuable things one can acquire in this life. Thus Proverbs teaches:

Get wisdom, get understanding; do not forget my words or swerve from them. Do not forsake wisdom, and she will protect you; love her, and she will watch over you. Wisdom is supreme; therefore get wisdom. Though it cost all you have, get understanding. (4:5–7)

Once we have humbled ourselves before the Creator and the creation and respect our human limits, our minds and hearts are freed to receive a kind of wisdom that will prosper us all the days of our earthly existence. Next to the wisdom revealed in Christ, this wisdom is the most valuable possession we can obtain.

This "wisdom for life" is the practical, earthly expression of the uncreated wisdom of God. It is characterized by an understanding of people, of the world and of day-to-day situations human beings face. This wisdom is bred of experience and observation. It is the product not only of personal reflection but embodies the reflections on life of countless, nameless generations of human beings from the beginning of human history. As part of the created order, it is available to anyone.[3] The common nature of wisdom should not blind believers to its basis in the uncreated wisdom of God.

The Virtue of Respectful Teachability

In order to receive and benefit from any kind of wisdom, we must be teachable. We must understand our human personal limitations, not think too highly of ourselves, and respect God and others. We think and act from the perspective that the created world has lessons to teach. We understand that human life, though externally different from the life of our forbearers, is lived by fallible human beings and governed by the same moral and practical laws applicable to former generations.

Not so long ago, a young person I know failed in a new job. This person was intelligent, well trained, likeable, and from a good family. Unfortunately, this person would not listen to good advice, however well meaning and however kindly given. This person was educated, but not teachable. We can never achieve wisdom by our own efforts and by our own capacity for learning. We have to be teachable. We have to let people and circumstances form our character so that we

---

3. Theologians distinguish between "common" and "natural" grace, the loving provision that God gives to everyone and "supernatural or saving grace," the special grace by which we know the true God and understand his provision for us in Christ.

become wise. Of course, the most important person to whom we must submit is God.

In submitting ourselves to God, to others, and to the witness of prior generations, we put ourselves in a position to become wise and avoid mistakes that have haunted human life throughout history. This is a hard attitude for people of contemporary thought to adopt. We are accustomed to thinking that all new ideas involve progress. We are inclined to think of the modern world as having escaped the superstitions of the past. We are likely to think in terms of our individual ideas, hopes, and dreams. We find it difficult to accept the notion that the past and our forbearers have important lessons to teach us—lessons that we ignore to our peril.

Habits of the Heart

The lessons of wisdom are not fully learned until they are made a part of our hearts and minds. Years ago, the sociologist Robert Bellah and his colleagues wrote an influential book called *Habits of the Heart*. The book was about the need to recover community and communitarian values in our society. The title speaks volumes about the deepest unmet need of our culture. We are inclined to believe that what we *know* is most important, as if mere knowledge is sufficient to change behavior. It is not. What we need is a *change of heart*.

In the Bible the "heart" is not just a pump that powers the circulatory system. It is the seat of our mind and emotions. The heart is where what we know, desire, and will meet in the unity of a human person. It is the center of our personality that powerfully guides who we are, who we become, the decisions we make, the instincts we follow, and the responses we make to circumstances. The change of heart we most need to be wise is a change induced by a changed relationship with God, with other people, and with God's creation.

Relational knowing and relational changes take time. Changes of heart normally do not occur in an instant, and when they do, there is often a long period of time before that change of heart is reflected in behavior. In fact, the deepest changes of our personality require both a change of mind and a change of behavior. This change of behavior finally results in a deep change in our personality.

One big challenge of our culture is to move from an untrammeled individualism to a deep sense of belonging to and being in communion with a spiritual, natural, and moral order. We also need to feel like we are part of a community formed in congruence with that order. Both the order of the world and the order of society are older, bigger, and wiser than we are. Humility and teachability are two of the most important qualities we can develop as human beings. It is a first step—and a big step—toward happiness and success in life.

Questions for Reflection

1. How would you describe the kind of awe and respect that leads to wisdom? How would you describe the result?

2. How are awe and humility related in our relationship with God? Can we really have awe and respect for God and not be humble towards God?

3. If we are humble and teachable, how does that affect our relationships with others? How does our behavior change when we are humbled?

4. John Templeton, founder of the Templeton Prize for Religion, wrote a book entitled *The Humble Approach*. How will we approach life and its problems if we are humble?

The Lord formed me from the beginning, before he created anything else. I was appointed in ages past, at the very first, before the earth began. I was born before the oceans were created, before the springs bubbled forth their waters. Before the mountains were formed, before the hills, I was born—before he had made the earth and fields and the first handfuls of soil. I was there when he established the heavens, when he drew the horizon on the oceans. I was there when he set the clouds above, when he established springs deep in the earth. I was there when he set the limits of the seas, so they would not spread beyond their boundaries. And when he marked off the earth's foundations, I was the architect at his side.

Proverbs 8:22–30a (NLT)

4

A Real, Personal Wisdom

For the biblical writers, practical and moral wisdom was *real*. The Bible teaches that the ultimate source and ground of wisdom is found in the reality of God. The notion of wisdom as something that exists outside of us, and to which we must conform, leads inevitably to the question, "So where does this wisdom come from?" For Christians, the ultimate source and ground of wisdom is the Triune God, Father, Son, and Holy Spirit.

If we are to conform to this source of wisdom in thinking and acting, it is important that we understand more about it and how we access it. The idea that wisdom, goodness, truth, and beauty have a reality outside of human choice runs contrary to our cultural formation. Most people today think of wisdom and morality as matters of social convention. Americans and Western Europeans tend to think of wisdom as whatever works in a given situation or culture. We do not see our moral decisions so much motivated by an order in the world as by our own desires and sense of what is best. The Bible acts as a powerful critique of our cultural assumptions in this area as in so many other areas of life.

Gwen is a graduate student at a major university. She grew up in a Christian home in the American Midwest. Gwen was a fine student in high school and in college. She grew up in a Christian home and was very active in her congregation's youth group. In college, Gwen was exposed to the radical skepticism found in the works of the philosopher Friedrich Nietzsche (1844–1900). As an English major she was exposed to the radical postmodern work of twentieth-century literary critics. In the end, she rejected her Christian faith. She simply felt that her faith was no longer defensible. Despite her rejection of Christianity, she does not find her new, secular faith fully satisfying. She cannot find a way to combine her new, postmodern worldview with her heart's yearning for a sense of "being at home in the universe."

Wisdom as the Active Agent in Creation

Our story—the Creation story—begins with a majestic prelude: "In the beginning, God created the heavens and the earth" (Gen 1:1). Proverbs teaches that the wisdom of God was "from the beginning" (Prov 8:22). The Bible explains that divine wisdom was active in God's rational creation of the universe (v. 30). As mentioned in the previous chapter, this wisdom is not described as a purely abstract mechanical wisdom. The God who is creating the world is a person engaged in a personal act of creation. For example, the New Testament teaches us that the divine wisdom revealed in Christ was present and through this wisdom the world was given its order (Col 1:16).

The creative wisdom of God is described in Proverbs in personal terms, so we read, "when he [God] marked off the earth's foundations, *I* was the architect at his side" (8:30a NLT; emphasis added). The use of personal language alerts us that God's wisdom is not merely a principle of order embedded in creation. The creating Wisdom of God is personal. As a person, wisdom cannot be known abstractly. It can only be known as part of a relationship, one characterized on the human side by faith, trust, and love.[1]

1. This is not the place to set out a full Trinitarian theology of wisdom. A way

Logos as Personal Being

The Apostle John begins his rendering of the story of Christ by affirming the identity of the wisdom Christ revealed with God: "In the beginning was the Word and the Word was with God, and the Word was God" (John 1:1). John goes on to identify this personal, relational being of the Word of God with Jesus, the Messiah, and the Logos (or "Word") of Greek philosophy. The Word of God that was with God in the beginning came and dwelt with us in human form, "full of unfailing love and faithfulness" in the person of Jesus the Christ (1:14 NLT).

The word we translate "Word" is the Greek word, "Logos." This word has a long history in Greek and Hebrew philosophy.[2] In Greek philosophy, the word "Logos" refers to the rational principle or reason behind the things that we see. In the Greek way of thinking, the physical universe was created by a rational principle. To the Hebrew way of thinking, this divine word or reason was part of the personal character of God. God did not just create the world as a divine mind. God did so as a divine character, and the world is meant to embody and reflect this character. God created the world through his own rational act and from the center of his own will and being.

The Apostle John and Christians understand the term "Word" to refer to the second person of the Trinity, who takes on human form in Jesus bar Joseph of the tiny town of Nazareth. In his gospel, John is saying that the principle of rational order in God became personally present to the human race in Jesus of Nazareth. Christ

of approaching the subject is to recognize that God is constituted in a relationship of divine self-giving love. Personhood and the communion among persons is not a secondary quality but constitute the being of God. See Zizioulas, *Being as Communion*, and Guyton, *Promise of Trinitarian Theology*.

2. Both the Greeks and Jewish philosophers like Philo of Alexandria employed this term to explain the nature of God. To the Greek, the "logos of a thing" is its inner reality, the rationality that pervades the created universe. See Kittel and Friedrich, "Logos," 506–7. In Greek philosophy it was a principle. Philo and other Hebrew thinkers gave it a personal dimension. John builds on their insight.

reveals the personal wisdom of God in human form—a form that we human beings can know through a personal encounter with God.[3] Paul identifies Christ with the uncreated wisdom of God saying, "He is the image of the invisible God, the firstborn over all creation. For by him all things were created: things in heaven and on earth, visible and invisible, whether thrones or powers or rulers or authorities; all things were created by him and for him" (Col 1:15–16).[4] The order of the world is finally founded in the orderliness of God who created it in love. This fusion of wisdom and love was revealed fully and finally in Jesus, the Christ.

Therefore, by the time the New Testament was complete its writers understood the wisdom of God as both *personal* and *relational*. The identification of wisdom with the Word incarnate in the person of Christ has important consequences: in Jesus of Nazareth the secret wisdom of God, his divine reason, was and is revealed and made public, so that anyone can come to know this wisdom in relationship with the One Word of God. This personal wisdom of God is ultimately to be known in a relationship of love because the One who created the world and all things within the world is a person who exists within a relationship of love, Father, Son, and Holy Spirit.

A Personal and Rational Creation

For biblical writers, creation is neither impersonal nor irrational. It has a purpose and an order. The world is the loving and wise creation of a personal Creator God, who embedded a loving divine rationality within it. Therefore, creation is not purposeless. In fact, creation's purpose is seen in the life, death, and resurrection of the One in whom and for whom it was created. Creation is not "over and

---

3. Brunner, *Christian Doctrine of God*, 26.

4. Wisdom is ultimately a personal revelation of the Word through which God created the world. Because the wisdom of God is essentially personal, just as God is essentially personal, it can only be known in a personal relationship of love.

against the human race," consisting of nothing but physical process and eventual futility.[5] The loving wisdom of God shines in the darkness of our world and of the human condition, giving life meaning and purpose.

Because God is personal, Christians do not believe that wisdom is discernible by disinterested abstract reason. Ultimate reality is not subject to our investigation by human reason alone or by the methods of science. Ultimate reality is not a principle or a thing, but a person of infinite rationality and self-giving relationality—a relationality we can only describe as self-giving love. Attempts to know God abstractly are bound to fail. God and the wisdom of God can only be known as any person is known—through a relationship. The specific relationship in which God can be known is a relationship of faith in which by grace God's love and wisdom are allowed to enter and transform a human soul.

Because God must be known personally, God cannot be known completely. Persons are by their very nature incapable of being fully understood by abstract reason. Those of us who have been married many years know that our spouses are fully capable of surprising us even in areas where we thought we understood them very well. Those who have raised children have had the same experience. Friends constantly do things we never imagined possible. To be a person is to have qualities that cannot be fully understood by any form of abstract or critical reason. Since God is the ultimate person, it should not surprise us that we cannot pretend to know God, even as well as we know our spouses, children and friends!

Because God cannot be known fully and finally by abstract reason, humility and a sense of our human limits is absolutely essential for the life of faith. What one learns within the relationship of humble faith is rational because the Creator has embedded within creation a kind of order that can be discerned as a person opens his or herself to the reality of God, the world, and other people. Nevertheless, in the end, we cannot fully comprehend the personal being of God. God is

5. Polkinghorne, *God of Hope*, 8–9.

beyond our full understanding—and so is God's creation. Religious wisdom inherently requires the humility of a trustful faith in the love and goodness of God.

The Realism of Wisdom Literature

Wisdom writers understood that God is real, the universe is real, and the moral order of the universe is real. They experienced God in worship, in their personal lives, and in the history of their nation. The Torah, the laws or teachings of God, were part of God's creation. The universe had a moral order—an order that was as real as the rocky hillsides of the Promised Land.

Sometimes we hear people speak of the moral order of the universe as "objective."[6] The Christian author C. S. Lewis speaks of the moral order as objective. In his essay, "Men Without Chests," Lewis critiques the modern subjectivist idea of morality, comparing it with what he calls the "Tao," which is the Way, the reality beyond reality, and the Way to which every human being should conform in order to act wisely. Here is how he describes the "Tao" or the moral order of the universe, what Christians might call the natural or moral law:

> It is the Way in which the universe goes on, the Way in which things everlastingly emerge, stilly and tranquilly, into space and time. It is also the way which every man should tread in imitation of that cosmic and supercosmic progression.[7]

Notice Lewis describes the order of the universe as both "cosmic," that is to say, a part of the created order, and "supercosmic," his way of saying transcendent or grounded in the ultimate reality of God. Conceived this way, the moral order is a part of creation yet grounded

6. Torrance, *Ground and Grammar of Theology*. Wisdom and the values wisdom discerns are "objective" in the sense of being "real," though their reality is different from that of physical reality. The reality of values is intellectual and spiritual, not physical and must be known in accordance with their reality.

7. Lewis, "Men without Chests," 28.

beyond the created order in the reality of its Creator. As such, morality is both part of the way things were meant to be (supercosmic) and a part of the way things in fact are (cosmic).

A moral order that is grounded in "how things are" is in some sense "objective." It cannot be denied or violated without a collision with the way things really are. Lewis goes on to say:

> And because our approvals and disapprovals are thus recognitions of objective value or responses to an objective order, therefore, emotional states can be in harmony with reason (when we feel liking for that which ought to be approved) or out of harmony with reason (when we perceive that liking is due but we cannot feel it).[8]

Many in our contemporary world, and especially those young people with a modern or postmodern affiliation, find it difficult to think of moral judgments and expressions of value as "objective." People with this mindset have been trained to think of faith and morals as subjective, and therefore, as matters of personal choice. We think of them arbitrarily as if we were simply choosing a flavor of ice cream.[9] Christians are bound to think of faith and morals in a different way. They are not "subjective" in the sense of being purely matters of personal choice. They are subjective in the sense of being personal appropriations of the revelation of a personal God. They are also objective because they are the revelations of a God who exists

---

8. Lewis, *Abolition of Man*, 29. The use by Lewis and others of the word "objective" is problematic for modern and postmodernists. We are inclined to think of things as objective when they can be perceived as a physical object. We instinctively think of things as being real as having this characteristic—they can be touched, felt, and measured. The kind of "objectivity" that religious and moral truths have is not the same as the objectivity of material objects, which is why I prefer the term "real."

9. Our modern world is deeply affected by a kind of subjective, "emotivist" (based solely on emotion) view of ethics and what we sometimes call "lifestyle issues." Matters of personal morality, sexual ethics, family formation, and a variety of other issues that prior generations thought were matters of reason, many in contemporary society now think of as matters of personal, subjective choice.

outside of us and who is the Creator of we human beings and the world we inhabit.

Even in everyday life, we do not act as if only visible, tangible reality is real and invisible realities are only matters of choice. Here is an example from my childhood. My father was a gardener, and our grass usually looked pretty good until he was too old to care for his lawn. As a child, I loved to lie down in the cool green grass in our yard on a clear spring night and look at the stars. I could feel the softness of the grass through my clothes. That grass was real. I could see and touch it. I saw its lovely, soft beauty. Eventually, I learned that the grass is made up of cells. Although I could not see those cells without a microscope, they were still real. Later on, I learned that those cells were in turn composed of atoms, which could only be detected with very sophisticated instruments. I believed in the reality of those atoms on the basis of what people of science considered true. Today, I know that atoms of which my lawn is composed are made up of electrons, protons, neutrons, and the like. These particles are themselves made up of bosons, mesons, and other particles that cannot be seen "objectively" in the normal way we use that word. Yet somehow, I believe they exist.

The point of my story is that we all "believe" in the reality of things that are unseen on the basis of the way in which those things explain the reality we directly experience. When someone says, "Taking drugs is foolish," pastors instinctively think of all the people, young and old, that we have seen injure, ruin, or even destroy their lives by taking drugs. My belief that taking drugs or drinking to excess is unwise is "objective" in the sense that it conforms to my experience of life—and the experiences of hundreds, thousands, even millions of other people over time. I also believe that the dangers I have observed will continue to manifest themselves in the future. The same thing can be said of most, if not all, practical, moral, and religious judgments we properly make.

The phrase "judgments we properly make" brings us to a final observation: our judgments are rarely absolutely final. This is true for several reasons. First, we are human and we sometimes make mistakes. This means I may make a moral judgment and on further reflection come to realize I was wrong. (I've done this many times in the past!) Second, we human beings are finite, so we are always discovering more about the world and about ethics and morals. Our understanding is always incomplete. Third, we all have our culturally conditioned way of looking at the world. The assumptions we bring to bear on any judgment can undermine our understanding of the reality of a situation. One of the values of education and travel is that we gain a capacity to see some of our own cultural limitations. This is true of Bible study. The fact that the world of the Bible is different than ours is helpful not hurtful. We know things that the biblical writers did not know—and they often know things we have forgotten or never knew.

Some people will read the previous paragraph and think, "Well, he has succumbed to moral relativism or subjectivity." This is not true. For example, the moral rule, "Thou Shalt Not Kill" is part of the order of the universe. Because violence is always fundamentally suspect, Christian and other traditions have developed what is sometimes called "Just War Theory." The idea behind Just War Theory is that some violence is justified, but only under specific circumstances. In approving of any given war, I might be wrong. I might have judged wrongly or simply have gotten my facts or logic wrong. I am finite and cannot know all that needs to be known.

One name for the position that I am outlining is "critical realism." When a person says that something is "real," he or she is confessing that it exists independently of their own subjective perceptions. To say that something such as "wisdom" exists independently of my perception of it and will impact my life whether or not I perceive it properly is to say that wisdom is "real" and "objective." As something that exists outside of my subjective preference, it will impact my life whether I subjectively recognize it or not.[10]

---

10. See, for example, Polanyi and Prosch, *Meaning*, 126. In Polanyi's thought, real things exist independently of any particular observer. We believe such

For biblical writers, the reality of human wisdom is finally grounded in the reality of uncreated personal wisdom of God. God's wisdom is not a mere extension of human wisdom. It is beyond any created wisdom, yet it is evident in creation (Rom 1:20). The Deep Wisdom of God is beyond our comprehension except by a revelation—a personal communication from God (1 Cor 2:6–7). This "speaking out" of wisdom is not private or hidden from human understanding.[11] It is revealed in everyday life, in the writings of wise people, in the revelation of Christ, in the Scriptures of the Old and New Testaments, and in tradition. For those who diligently seek wisdom, it will continue to reveal itself in the future under many different circumstances.

A Personal Wisdom Embedded in Creation

The kind of wisdom we need for daily living is both natural (embedded in the world) and supernatural (grounded in God beyond the natural order of the world). The writers of Proverbs capture this personal character of wisdom when they personify wisdom as a woman crying out to the human race to pay attention. For example, Proverbs 8 describes wisdom as a lady crying out to foolish people who ignore her:

> Does not wisdom call, and does not understanding raise her voice? On the heights, beside the way, at the crossroads she takes her stand; beside the gates in front of the town, at the entrance of the portals she cries out: "To you, O people, I call, and my cry is to all that live." (vv. 1–4 NRSV)

things will manifest themselves in the future in the same and similar situations.

11. Wisdom literature often portrays wisdom as a person who "cries out" and lectures the human race as it passes by her day after day without responding (see Prov 2:20–21).

Wisdom reveals itself as a personal reality calling out to us in the midst of the concrete circumstances of life.[12]

Wisdom literature teaches that God embedded this wisdom within creation, even within human relationships. Not only does revelation require compliance with that order, but human reason is capable of understanding it and human will is capable of acting on that wisdom. For example, the sanctity of marriage, and likewise the danger of adultery, is not just a matter of divine law; it is also a matter of common sense that anyone ought to be able to deduce from simple observation (Prov 7:6–27). This is why Paul in Romans can say that human beings are without excuse when violating the moral law because the nature of the unseen wisdom is reflected in and discernible from the creation God has made (Rom 1:19–20).

This aspect of wisdom is what in Christian terms we call the "natural law." Embedded in a Christian notion of "natural law" is the idea that the Creator embedded in human beings a character that can be discovered and conformed to in order to live wisely. It is the conviction of the writers of the wisdom tradition that morals are "written on the heart" of human beings, as difficult as it may be to discern their precise application in particular situations.[13]

This notion is deeply at odds with what much of what our culture teaches. Many people, under the pressure of the cultural presuppositions of our society, have lost their intuitive ability to recognize the reality of ideas, such as "right" and "wrong" or "wise" and "foolish." Too many people have ceased participating in the long tradition of Western thought that believes that values are real. The reality of wisdom and values is different than the reality of a chair or a table, but they are real and they have the ability to determine our destiny.

Modern society often creates a kind of disconnect between the outer life of a person in the world and the inner life of that person.

---

12. Wisdom cries out in the practical and moral areas of life, just as the heavens cry out in Psalm 19:1–4, where the author says that the heavens cry out speaking to humanity without a sound, revealing the order of creation.

13. See Budziszeweski, *Written on the Heart*, 61.

The outer world is real and objective. The inner world is personal and subjective. This is a key reason why many people think one way and live another. Such people eventually develop a deep schism of the soul. The outer person is a kind of ever-changing mask covering a certain type of emptiness. Pastors and counselors see the results of that disconnect every day.

A constant phenomenon of the contemporary religious scene is that many people are completely capable of thinking that something is "unbiblical" or even "wrong" but still engage in such behaviors in their personal life. For example, many Christians say that premarital sex or divorce for convenience is wrong or unbiblical, while practicing such behaviors. A disconnect between what people believe to be true and how they in fact behave is psychologically and socially unhealthy.

The way of wisdom begins with a profound faith that the world is orderly and rewards those who seek to understand and live according to its order. This faith results in an ability to achieve unity between the inner and outer self that is consistent with a kind of "relationality" embedded in creation that includes physical, moral, and spiritual components. The inner reality of the human soul and its outer expression in human behavior are then bound together by the moral character of the universe.

People in today's modern world are often described as "alienated." One benefit of the older, wisdom tradition is that human beings can feel "at home in the universe"—which was made with us in mind and with the potential for us to have orderly lives. Because we are part of the loving and rational creation of a loving and rational God, we are ultimately at home in the universe. This "at homeness" does not eliminate the reality of sin, of brokenness, of evil, or the results of our finitude. It does mean that we are in some sense deeply a part of and at home in the universe God created.

In Proverbs, Lady Wisdom not only cries out, she also prepares a *home* for those who respond to her call:

Wisdom has built her house, she has hewn her seven pillars. She has slaughtered her animals, she has mixed her wine, she has also set her table. She has sent out her servant-girls, she calls from the highest places in the town, "You that are simple, turn in here!" To those without sense she says "Come, eat of my bread and drink of the wine I have mixed. Lay aside immaturity, and live, and walk in the way of insight." (9:1–6 NRSV)

There is more at stake in God's agency in creation than we commonly imagine. Part of what is at stake is our capacity to find a place in creation—a place we can call our home. The home that wisdom builds in this world is a home that is in some way fit for those who inhabit it.

Modern science reveals a universe that is both deeply *rational* and deeply *relational*. Relativity theory, quantum theory, and chaos theory all portray a world of inherent relationality and inherent order. Form and being, theory and reality, the outer perceptible thing and the inner rules of its existence and behavior exist in a delicate relationship. The world is deeply connected both at a subatomic and at an everyday level of life. In such a world, the smallest input of energy or information, the most insignificant act of love or hatred, can have dramatic consequences.[14]

Such a world is just the kind of world that a God of Deep Love (Relationality) and Deep Light (Rationality) might create. In such a world, as terrifying as it may be on occasion, human beings can find more than meaningless existence. We can find a home.[15] The world is the good creation of a good God who personally loves us in a sacrificial and unconditional way. Such a God would only create a world with a natural and moral order within which his beloved creatures

14. The term "relationality" expresses the idea of creation as inherently relational. That is, all things are bound together. In the end, this relationality extends as deeply as we can pierce into the universe. For an interesting and illuminating examination of the implications of an entangled world, see Polkinghorne, *Trinity and an Entangled World*.

15. Polkinghorne, *Faith of a Physicist*.

could find a home. This home is not ultimately unknowable and unlike us. It is in fact made with us in mind. By living in communion with the world and the One who created it, we can achieve wisdom and find happiness and joy.

There is an old gospel hymn called "Softly and Tenderly," which speaks of this in the traditional language of faith:

> Softly and tenderly, Jesus is calling:
> Calling for you and for me.
> See on the portals he's waiting and watching,
> Watching for you and for me.
> Come home. Come home.
> Ye who are weary come home.
> Earnestly, tenderly Jesus is calling,
> Calling, "O Sinner, come home!"

The voice of wisdom is ultimately a voice calling us to come home from a frantic life of self-seeking to the order and love of life lived in accordance with the love and wisdom of the One who created the heavens and the earth.

Questions for Reflection

1. What does wisdom literature teach us about the role Wisdom played in creation?

2. If Proverbs teaches us that wisdom is from God, what other quality does God have relative to his creation? (Ps 135:5–10; 145:12; 147:5)

3. In what ways do you consider your moral and lifestyle decisions as matters of personal choice and in what ways do you sense in them an unfolding discovery?

4. What does it mean to be "at home in the universe"?

My child, do not forget my teaching, but let your heart keep my command-ments; for length of days and years of life and abundant welfare they will give you. Do not let loyalty and faithfulness forsake you; bind them round your neck, write them on the tablet of your heart. So you will find favor and good repute in the sight of God and of people. Trust in the Lord with all your heart, and do not rely on your own insight. In all your ways acknowledge him, and he will make straight your paths.

PROVERBS 3:1–6 (NRSV)

5

The Parental Voice of Wisdom

From whom are human beings to learn the skill of living wisely? Like any skill, it cannot be learned from a book. It must be learned from someone who already possesses the skill. Throughout life, we need teachers and mentors if we are to become wise and skilled in any area. Mentors are people we can watch, learn from, and imitate as we develop our personal skills. Our first mentors in the skill of living are, or should be, our parents and family members.

Over and over again, Proverbs begins with an exhortation using the narrative voice of a concerned and loving parent. For example in Proverbs 4:

> Listen, children, to a father's instruction, and be attentive, that you may gain insight; for I give you good precepts: do not forsake my teaching. When I was a son with my father, tender, and my mother's favorite, he taught me, and said to me, "Let your heart hold fast my words; keep my commandments, and live. Get wisdom; get insight: do not forget, nor turn away from the words of my mouth. Do not forsake her, and she will keep you; love her, and she will guard you." (vv. 1–6 NRSV)

Throughout wisdom literature, wisdom writers speak as a parent attempting to impart wisdom to children. Often, there is a sense of urgency—the resolve of one who deeply desires to impart a most important lesson to a beloved child. The representative parent is desperately attempting to see that the child has the wisdom and life skills necessary to meet the difficulties of life. In Proverbs, the voice of the parent urges children to hold fast to the commandments of the parent and to learn the wisdom necessary to apply the parent's teachings to the problems of daily life. Such wisdom is the most important thing a parent can impart to a child. It is more important than any material possession (Prov 3:14).

Most of us understand that a primary duty of parents is to pass along to children the knowledge, skills, and character needed to meet life's challenges. The writers of wisdom literature assume that a well-ordered household will contain a mother and a father, both of whom accept responsibility for teaching and caring for their children.[1] In the culture from which wisdom literature emerged, it also would have been normal to have grandparents and others living in the household and interacting with children.

The parental voice of wisdom embodies a worldview in which wisdom and foolishness, good and evil, and the like are active forces in the universe. Moral goodness impacts relationships and behavior. Relationships and behavior determine success and failure in life. Therefore, wisdom allows a person to successfully meet the moral and therefore the practical challenges of life (4:8–9). Wisdom prevents mistakes that can cause failure in life (v. 12). In particular, wisdom imparts the ability to resist the temptation to violence and wickedness (vv. 14–17).

Children and youth are by their nature shortsighted. They have not lived long enough to appreciate the long-term consequences of their actions. Good parents impress upon their children the impact of evil and foolish behavior on their future happiness and the blessings associated with righteous behavior. Perhaps more importantly, good parents model wise behavior for their children so that they can see and emulate what it means to live a wise life and face its challenges successfully.

1. Toy, "Proverbs," 133.

In Deuteronomy, Moses teaches the people:

> Now this *is* the commandment, *and these are* the statutes and judgments which the Lord your God has commanded to teach you, that you may observe *them* in the land which you are crossing over to possess, that you may fear the Lord your God, to keep all His statutes and His commandments which I command you, you and your son and your grandson, all the days of your life, and that your days may be prolonged. Therefore hear, O Israel, and be careful to observe *it,* that it may be well with you, and that you may multiply greatly as the Lord God of your fathers has promised you—"a land flowing with milk and honey." Hear, O Israel: The Lord our God, the Lord *is* one! You shall love the Lord your God with all your heart, with all your soul, and with all your strength. And these words which I command you today shall be in your heart. You shall teach them diligently to your children, and shall talk of them when you sit in your house, when you walk by the way, when you lie down, and when you rise up. You shall bind them as a sign on your hand, and they shall be as frontlets between your eyes. You shall write them on the doorposts of your house and on your gates. (Deut 6:1–9 NKJV)

Moses's command to the people of Israel represents an understanding that children need parents who pass on the religious, moral, and cultural norms to their children. If they do so, their lives will be blessed.

In contemporary society, people often think that children will "naturally" (i.e., without education, training, example, and discipline) learn the habits and virtues needed to confront the difficulties and challenges of life. Parents are often involved in their own journey of self-discovery or self-fulfillment and leave children without guidance. This results in many children feeling lost and rootless.

Gloria is sitting alone in her bedroom at home. Her mother and stepfather are out for dinner. Gloria's biological father left her mother when she was quite young. After a few years as a single, her mother remarried. Both her mother and stepfather work, and they have two children together. Her biological father has also remarried and spends little time with his daughter. Her grades, never good, have recently become worse, and her mother has been angry at her lack of attention at school. Gloria's parents do not attend church, and she has no youth pastor or other adult with whom she is close. Gloria feels alone and lonely, without guidance at this very difficult time of her life.

In fact, children and youth need exposure to the life experience of parents and of all those who have gone before them in the difficult and sometimes frustrating business of living. Wise living requires a long process of character formation. This formation requires active involvement of people with character who invest time, energy, and love in forming the character of children. Parents are best positioned to perform this difficult task. Parents have (or should have) constant, daily opportunity and ability to share their wisdom and experience with their children.

One common observation of teachers, pastors, and others concerns the extent to which contemporary parents turn over their parental responsibilities to schools, churches, youth leaders, teachers, and others. Although teachers, pastors, volunteers, and others are happy to help with children, and often invest much time in trying to help troubled youth, they are no substitute for involved parents. Professionals just do not have the time and personal presence necessary to impart faith to children and youth without parents being the primary source of spiritual and moral formation.

Over and over again pastors are confronted with parents who have not regularly brought their children to church and have not insisted that they regularly participate in youth activities. When a crisis comes, such parents sometimes feel that the church has failed them. Sometimes we have. More often, we have simply not had the opportunity to get to know and understand the child so that we can help them. Sometimes that parent is actually engaging in the activity they find objectionable in their child, such as using recreational drugs. In such circumstances neither the church or teachers in school, nor others can overcome the failure of parents to take responsibility for the raising of their own children.

The Voice of the Experience of the Human Race

Behind the parental voice in Proverbs is another parental voice—the voice of the wisdom of the ages. This voice of wisdom is the embodiment of the experience of generations of human beings over thousands of years. This voice speaks from the entire experience of the human race. The successes and failures of countless generations of men and women are embodied in the teachings of wisdom literature. When a parent encourages a child to work hard in school, he or she speaks as the embodied voice of generation after generation of human beings who have faced and sometimes succumbed to laziness. The voice is not just the voice of a single parent or other authority figure. It is the voice of every parent who ever lived; all the loving and wise parents who have sought to spare their children the bitterness of failure and loss.

This intergenerational, intercultural voice contained in wisdom literature is the voice of the collective wisdom of the human race from its emergence until the present day. This voice is made up of the experience of countless thousands of human beings as they confronted concrete problems of life. The pithy, short sayings of Proverbs, the difficult story of Job, the meditations of Ecclesiastes, all represent that voice speaking through the experience of the Jewish people at particular points in their history. Each time the parental voice is heard, it is at one and the same time the voice of a cultural and religious tradition that extends to the very beginning of the human race.[2]

This intergenerational voice needs to be heard not just by children and young adults, but by everyone. That is why in the very beginning of Proverbs the writer is careful to say that adults, even the wisest adults, need to hear the voice of wisdom (1:5). No one can possibly carry around all the wisdom and understanding they need for all of life. In order to live wisely, adults must continue to return to the well of wisdom and draw deeply from its depths in order to meet the challenges of life.

It can be difficult for people in this Modern Age to hear that voice with the proper combination of attentiveness and respect for the wisdom of those who have gone before. The Modern Age (beginning about three hundred years ago) was and is characterized by hostility to tradition and especially to religious and moral traditions that cannot be verified within the narrow and inadequate definition of reason employed by many modern thinkers.[3] Our age does not celebrate the careful inheritor of a tradition. Instead, we celebrate the individual who breaks with tradition, refusing to accept a moral code or lifestyle simply because their tradition recommends it. Our extreme individualism finds its final expression in the often-repeated phrase, "Just because it is true (or right) for you does not mean that it is true (or right) for me."

2. The American philosopher Charles S. Pierce, the founder of pragmatism, that most American of all philosophies, put it this way: "The catholic (universal) consent that constitutes the truth is by no means limited to men in this earthly life or to the entire human race, but extends to the whole communion of minds to which we belong, including some whose senses are very different than ours." Pierce, "Works of George Berkeley—1871," 60.

3. Beginning with the Enlightenment, philosophers often reduced knowledge to (i) that which was deducible by logic or mathematical reason (so-called "a priori" truth or truths of reason) and (ii) synthetic truths or truths of direct and verifiable experience. Religious truths and truths of historical experience did not easily meet this standard. One benefit of the emergence of postmodernism is the end of this constricted view of reason.

Careful thinkers recognize that we are exiting the Modern Age and entering another period of human history. In science and in other disciplines, many thinkers recognize that in every human endeavor there is a tradition at work. The philosopher of science Michael Polanyi has described how every scientist inevitably functions as part of a tradition of truth seeking based upon the commitment of science to the foundational belief that the world is orderly and can be systematically described and understood.[4] In order to discover any truth, including scientific truth, we must join a community of people who are trying to find the truth we are interested in knowing. We apprentice ourselves to those who know more than we know.

Just for a moment, let's suppose that the truth you want to discover involves the cause of cancer. Let's suppose you have this moment of self-realization just before first grade. To become a scientist, you will pay attention to your teachers throughout grade school years, especially where math and science are concerned. Then, you will study biology, chemistry, and physics in high school. You will probably take Biology II if it is offered. Then, when you get to college, you will take many, many more courses in biology, chemistry, and the like. Most of the time, you will be taking courses far afield from your direct interest, but you will be learning to think like a scientist. After four years of college, you will go to graduate school and/or medical school and spend many years apprenticing with scientists in your chosen field. Finally, after those years of apprenticeship you will begin your work at the forefront of your chosen field.[5]

The same thing is true in any field of knowledge—religious, moral, legal, or otherwise—as well as in the business of life: to make progress in any field of inquiry we must apprentice ourselves to those who have preceded us. In any field of endeavor, we must commit ourselves in faith to those with whom we study. In my example above,

4. Michael Polanyi elaborates this understanding of the nature of science especially in his works, *Personal Knowledge* and *Science, Faith and Society*.

5. This illustration was suggested to me by Leslie Newbigin's work, see his *Gospel in a Pluralist Society*, 44–45.

the student trusts that his or her teachers in biology understand the field and are capable of teaching the subject. In the beginning the student takes as given the skills and understandings of scientists in a field of study. The student begins by repeating experiments that practitioners in their chosen field have already done. As a student goes on in preparing for a future scientific career, he or she commits to a group of scientists with whom he or she will do research and whose approach to the problem the student will follow.

The necessity to commit to a tradition is applicable to success in the endeavor of life as well as in science. We begin life (hopefully) with a loving family. For a long time, we obey our parents, learn their values, and internalize their virtues without thinking. During our early years, we learn to obey reasonable requests, to take care of ourselves, to avoid danger and dangerous situations, to work hard at chores that are the beginning of our work ethic. This period lasts a long time, but it is not time wasted, for it carries within it the building blocks of our character.

Eventually, often in our teen years, we begin to make our own choices, applying the principles our parents and others taught us. This is a time of trial and error (an experience every parent dreads). We still need our parents, teachers, and other mentors, for we are still young. Finally, we reach adulthood. We still listen to our parents and mentors, but we have become adults, responsible for our own choices and ready to make them. Eventually, we have children and the cycle repeats itself. The period of apprenticeship is an important period in any endeavor, but perhaps most of all in the endeavor of life.

Polanyi speaks of the value of "maxims" or "rules of art."[6] Such maxims cannot be learned in the absence of practicing the art. For example, it is no use just reading books on the art of golfing. One has to play golf to understand the value of the rules of golf and how to put them into practice. One can't learn to knit just by reading books on knitting. One has to practice knitting, often with someone who has mastered the skill.

6. See Polanyi, *Personal Knowledge*, 30–31.

What is true of any scientific, athletic, or other skill is even truer when it comes to the skill of living wisely. The skillful practitioner of life, who confronts the problems of life with good judgment, must not only know the wisdom of his or her forbearers, but must also learn that wisdom by facing the universal problems of life in the context of a particular culture and time. This is one reason why our need for wisdom and for mentoring never ends: we are always confronting new challenges and needing new and deeper wisdom to succeed at life.

Wisdom literature reflects many and varied human responses to critical situations that human beings face in life. It is a sourcebook for maxims and rules of art that enable a person to be a successful practitioner of the "game of life." This literature also explores character traits human beings possess or fail to possess that determine success or failure. Wisdom literature does not provide all the answers to the problems we will face in life. It does provide us with general principles and an approach to problems and choices. It also provides a way of thinking, and habits of thought and action, that hold us in good stead throughout the various pressures and difficulties of life.

Wisdom literature provides us access to parables, poems, maxims, and the like that function like mental tools.[7] These poems, parables, maxims, and sayings represent a received wisdom, a kind of "folk wisdom" that represents the experience of generations of people who, in different cultures and in different situations, faced many of the same problems we face.[8] In raising, teaching, and mentoring young people, it is important to help them by providing them with "proverbial and other mental tools" that can be used in various situations as a basis for personal judgment.

7. Ibid., 55–57. Polanyi shows that our minds use words and concepts like tools to explore a reality. Just as a doctor uses a probe to examine a patient with his or her attention focused on the patient, humans use words to explore reality with our focus on the problem we are trying to understand.

8. Ibid., 58–59. "We are faced here with the general principle by which our beliefs are anchored in ourselves. Hammers and probes can be replaced by intellectual tools, think of any interpretive framework" (59).

Not so long ago, I was counseling a young person involved in a business negotiation. The person was considering a bluffing tactic about which he or she had some ethical qualms. In the course of our discussion, it occurred to me that the other side of the negotiation might easily know the bluff was a bluff. Therefore, I said, "It is never a good idea to bluff if the other players have seen your cards." Almost immediately the young person understood that not only was the bluff potentially unethical, it was also potentially foolish. This little saying of the moment is an example of a proverb with many applications that can lead a person to a wise way of evaluating a situation. It is a kind of maxim that does not make a decision for a person, but leads that person to a wise decision.

Life is not a science. Living is more like an art or skill. Because living involves skill, it can only be learned from watching and internalizing the expertise of others who are further along the journey of life. In speaking of learning artful skills generally, Polanyi makes this important observation:

> An art which cannot be specified in detail cannot be transmitted by prescription, since no prescription for it exists. It can be passed only by example from master to apprentice.[9]

One reason parenting is so important is that wise living is not a subject like abstract mathematics that can be taught in a classroom. Wise living is an art that must be passed on from generation to generation in personal relationships, between those who are more experienced, and those who are less so. This is one reason why so-called "values curriculum" in schools have been sometimes disappointing. They are good in and of themselves, but they are no substitute for the personal relationship of a parent or mentor and a child.

9. Ibid., 53.

Getting our Vision Right

This observation leads to an analogy Calvin uses in his *Institutes of the Christian Religion*. Earlier we spoke of proverbial literature as "mental tools," short memorable sayings and stories that allow us to probe situations wisely and react to them in ways that are life enhancing. There is a sense in which reading and internalizing wisdom literature changes the way we see the world, just as a scientific advance, like the Theory of Relativity, changed the way we see the world. In biblical wisdom literature we are putting on the spectacles of God so that we can see reality as God sees it.

In his *Institutes of Religion*, John Calvin likens the role of Scripture to the role of eyeglasses:

> Just as old or bleary-eyed men and those with weak vision, if you thrust before them a most beautiful volume, even if they seem to be some sort of writing, yet they can scarcely construe two words, but with the aid of spectacles will begin to read distinctly; so Scripture, gathering up the otherwise confused knowledge of God in our minds, having dispersed our dullness, clearly shows us the true God.[10]

Scripture, including wisdom literature, functions as "reading glasses for life," illuminating not just human wisdom but that wisdom only God can reveal to us.

As we read and internalize the teachings of wisdom, we learn a new way of looking at the world. Our vision of life is sharpened and corrected. We learn to look at the world and its problems with humility instead of pride. We learn to look at those less fortunate with love instead of disdain. We learn to focus on respecting and loving others instead of on our personal human desires. Instead of looking at the world as immature humans, we learn to look at the world through the eyes of God.

10. Calvin, *Institutes of the Christian Religion*, 70.

From Parent to Child

There is a place where wisdom is to be learned—first in our biological family, then in our cultural family, but finally in the family of God. We can learn to be shrewd in a worldly way without joining the family of faith, but the wisdom of an Abraham, Moses, or Jesus cannot be learned without joining the family of faith. It is in this family—the family of God—that we meet the parent and mentor we will need not just while we are young but throughout all of life.

The kind of learning required to become wise only partially involves learning principles. There is a need to learn, memorize, and internalize principles, but there is more. The principles must also be applied to a variety of ever changing circumstances within a specific society and culture at a particular point in its history. This requires a constant interplay between an individual, a context, and the principles of wisdom applicable to a specific situation.

In a way, learning to live wisely is similar to learning to putt in the game of golf. Putting is a fairly simple physical act if all one considers is the actual movement of the arms and wrists. However, since every green is different and every angle of every putt is different, that simple physical act must be practiced, watched, evaluated, and adapted to an always-changing environment. Developing such a skill requires mentoring—and the game of life is infinitely more complex than golf.

Questions for Reflection

1. Did your parents or some other adult attempt to teach you how to live wisely? Who? How has your upbringing impacted your life?

2. In what ways does it help you to understand why guidance is important in life when you think of wisdom literature as embodying a parental wisdom gradually built up over all of human history?

3. Does the idea of wisdom equipping you with mental tools to face the challenges of life help you see the importance of wisdom? Why or why not?

4. Do you think your moral and lifestyle decisions have resulted in part from a worldview? Up to now, what view of the world has informed your decision-making? How would believing that Scripture, and wisdom literature in general, is "God breathed" change the way you think of wisdom?

The path of the righteous is like the first gleam of dawn, shining ever brighter till the full light of day. But the way of the wicked is like deep darkness; they do not know what makes them stumble.

PROVERBS 4:18–19

6

The Two Ways

Life involves a Choice of Paths

We do not often walk at night without any light, but in the ancient world, people did. It is hard for us to understand the danger and the fear of being alone in the wilderness on a dark night and vulnerable to dangerous beasts—and even more dangerous human beings. Many years ago as a Boy Scout, I forgot my flashlight and had to make my way at night across a ridge and through a valley while returning to the main camp. Once down in the valley, there was barely any moonlight. It was difficult, even impossible, not to make wrong turns and become lost. The hike was a nervous and harrowing one—and I was very glad when I saw the light of the dining hall in the distance. The memory of the small amount of fear and danger of that evening, when I might have lost my way, has never left me. Imagine then the terror a person might feel in the vast wastelands of the ancient world. Imagine the fear ancient, Middle Eastern Bedouins experienced if they went astray in the desert at night with no light or path to guide their way.

In the modern world we have lost the sense that moral laws and the wisdom of the ages create a kind of beacon—a light in the darkness of the uncertainties and difficulties of life. As we pay attention to the experience and teachings of those who have gone before us, we internalize the tools we need in order to navigate the problems of life. But the mental tools we receive are only tools; we must apply them.

Life is a series of choices. Day in and day out we decide what course of action we are going to take—what path we are going to follow—in a variety of situations. The character of our decisions depends not only on what we know but also upon our experience and our character. C. S. Lewis describes the importance of the decisions we make this way:

> Every time you make a choice you are turning the central part of you, the part that chooses, into something a little different than it was before.[1]

Whether we want to believe it or not, every choice we make in life determines our character. These choices are often far from neutral. Our choices determine whether we are going to be a self-centered or other-centered person. Our choices determine whether we will be a thoughtful person or an impulsive person. Our choices take us nearer to happiness and wholeness or they take us further away. Choices matter because choices determine who we are and who we become.

Developing the capacity to make good decisions concerning the directions we will take in life, the paths we will follow, and the company we will keep is the most important capacity and talent we can have. If we do not develop the capacity to make good choices and follow the best path, we wander through life ending up further and further from the happiness and wholeness we desire for our loved ones and ourselves.

Paths of Righteousness and Wickedness

The writers of wisdom literature describe the most basic choice human beings make as a choice between two ways of life. These two

1. Lewis, *Mere Christianity*, 82.

ways are described as the choice between the "path of wisdom" and the "path of foolishness." On other occasions, they are described as the "path of the righteous" and the "path of the wicked." The first path leads to life, wholeness, and happiness; the other leads to frustration, failure, and death. Early in Proverbs, the writers set out the choice young people must make between the "path of light" and the "path of darkness" and what is at stake in the decision. The result of following the path of darkness is calamity, destruction—even death (Prov 1:27, 32). The result of following the path of light is success in solving the problems of life, protection in times of trouble, and salvation from evil persons (2:7, 12–17).

The image of the light path of wisdom and the dark path of foolishness or evil is repeated over and over again. For example, "The path of the righteous is like the first gleam of dawn, shining ever brighter till the full light of day. But the way of the wicked is like deep darkness; they do not know what makes them stumble" (4:18–19). Living wisely leads to a bright future. Foolish and unrighteous living ultimately leads to a dark future of frustration and failure. The Way of the One Who Is and Will Be is a Way of Light, of life, and blessing. Those who travel on the paths of God act wisely, receive protection along the journey of life, and blessing at life's completion. Those who fail to travel that way, travel "against the grain of the universe" and find only ruin and pain. Therefore, the wisdom writers observe, "The way of the Lord is a refuge for the righteous, but it is the ruin of those who do evil" (10:29).

What is the way of righteousness that leads to abundant life? It is a life the contours of which are set by the teachings contained in the Old and New Testaments. For the Jew, the righteous life is a life lived in conformity with the Torah, which is sometimes translated as the "Law" but might as accurately be translated "teaching" or "instruction." The path of a righteous person is characterized by following the Torah (the Law or the instructions of God). Following the Torah places one on a path that leads to blessing. On the other hand, one who is not righteous does not follow the Law and ends up stumbling through life. That person is traveling on a path that leads to failure. For Christians, the path of life is found by accepting God's gift of salvation from the forces of darkness and following the teachings and example of Jesus Christ whom we believe fully embodied the Way of life. In both cases, it is a life guided by the narrative and teachings transmitted by the writers of Holy Scripture.

Learning to distinguish the path of light from the path of darkness is one of the most important functions of wisdom literature. Thus:

> Wisdom will save you from the ways of wicked men, from men whose words are perverse, who leave the straight paths to walk in dark ways, who delight in doing wrong and rejoice in the perverseness of evil, whose paths are crooked and who are devious in their ways. (2:12–15)

The wise person avoids the "dark path" of wickedness and follows the "lighted path" illuminated by wisdom. To enjoy the benefits of the path of light, one must choose the path of righteousness and wisdom.

Paths of Wisdom and Foolishness

There is a second path wisdom literature warns young people against following—the path of folly. One feature of Proverbs is the personification of wisdom and foolishness as two different sorts of women. Often, "lady wisdom" is compared and contrasted with "the foolish lady." Lady Wisdom and Lady Folly are seen as competing for the attention of the human race. Early in Proverbs we hear wisdom speaking in the public streets of an ancient village:

> Wisdom calls aloud in the street, she raises her voice in the public squares; at the head of the noisy streets she cries out, in the gateways of the city she makes her speech: "How long will you simple ones love your simple ways? How long will mockers delight in mockery and fools hate knowledge?" (1:20–22)

Lady Wisdom leads her followers down the path of wisdom. She builds a home that is affluent and secure.

Lady Folly, on the other hand, attracts her followers and leads them down a path of destruction and death:

> The woman named Folly is brash. She is ignorant and doesn't know it. She sits in her doorway on the heights overlooking the city. She calls out to men going by who are minding their own business. "Come in with me," she urges the simple. To those who lack good judgment, she says, "Stolen water is refreshing; food eaten in secret tastes the best!" But little do they know that the dead are there. Her guests are in the depths of the grave. (9:13–18 CEV)

There is a particular kind of person—the kind of person wisdom literature describes as "the fool." The fool does not listen to the sometimes demanding call of Lady Wisdom; instead he or she listens to the siren song of Lady Folly. This kind of person habitually lacks self-discipline and ignores good advice. Fools are often "mockers," that is they not only ignore good advice and traditional morals, they actually make fun of wisdom and righteousness (Prov 30:17). The fool listens to bad advice, gives little heed to wisdom, follows his or her passions, and does not respect the moral law. Such people live on the basis of passing desire, momentary impulse, and fad. The path they are taking seems attractive and life enhancing, but the end of their journey is failure and death.

Ellie is a "latch key child." Her father and mother divorced when she was young. Her father soon remarried and moved to a different city. Ellie's mother works hard and takes Ellie to church regularly. Nevertheless, she has a social life and is looking for a partner with whom she can share her life. As a result, Ellie spends a good bit of time at home with her older brother and sister. Ellie has grown into a lovely young lady, but she is vulnerable to any male who shows her appreciative attention. She is inclined to make poor choices. Recently, she began dating an older boy, and they have become intimate. They have been drinking and partying together—and Ellie has begun to take recreational drugs with him. Ellie has begun to make poor choices. Her mother, when she discovers what Ellie is doing, will be devastated.

Most unfortunately, our culture encourages people to make poor, shortsighted choices, and there are plenty of people around to encourage foolish behavior. Movies, music, and much of popular media make fun of traditional morals. Government and academia are filled with such persons. There is a widespread assumption that traditional faith and traditional mores are outmoded, life denying, and useless. In such a culture, it is not surprising that many, many young people find themselves on a path that cannot help but result in suffering and pain. In such a culture it can be difficult and sometimes dangerous to suggest that the ideas of those who make fun of traditional virtues are themselves foolish.

The Motivation for Our Choices

Human beings always make motivated decisions. We decide what to value and what to do based upon our perception of the advantages and disadvantages of a particular choice. We normally choose the path we think will lead to our happiness, one way or another. Many of the motivations for our choices are unconscious and may involve our human brokenness. Consequently, it is important for us to be conscious of our motivations and control them. Some of our conscious motivations are in fact mistaken, and they need to be corrected. Making choices is complex and demands both knowledge of the facts and knowledge about ourselves.

The psalmist declares that those who follow the path of wisdom, those who meditate day and night upon the instructions of God, are like trees planted by a stream of clear, pure water (Ps 1:3). Because such trees receive proper nourishment, they bear fruit at the proper time. Foolish people are not like this. They are like trees planted in a desert. Eventually, they dry up and die (v. 4). There are many other descriptions of the importance of good decisions in wisdom literature. The purpose of these many descriptions of the consequences of both wise and foolish behavior is to motivate readers to choose wisely. The person who meditates on wisdom develops the habit of resisting dysfunctional, unwise impulses, thinks through decisions and their consequences, and acts accordingly. Foolish people are brash and unthinking, motivated by short-term pleasure seeking, and do not habitually think through the long-term consequences of decisions.

Over the years, congregations that I have served as a layperson and as a pastor devoted a lot of time and energy to Bible study. It is important for Christians to have an overall idea of what the Bible says from Genesis to Revelation. It is also important for Christians to understand the principles upon which Christians make decisions. It is important for Christians to understand how to wisely use Scripture to seek daily wisdom for living. The Bible is a book for discipleship, for spiritual formation, and for guiding action; it is not primarily a document for abstract scholarly study. Christians need to develop an understanding of the world that inclines them to make life decisions based upon a wise foundation in God. Our notion of what does and does not constitute happiness and fulfillment needs to be formed by Scripture so that our choices are made with a proper motivation.

A Worldview Formed by Wisdom

In the last chapter, we spoke of an analogy that Calvin uses, the analogy of "spectacles." Those of us who have glasses look at the world through the corrective lenses through which we need to see the world more clearly. For Calvin, Scripture is the chosen means by which God corrects our spiritual and moral vision so that we see the world as God sees it. To make wise decisions, we need to have our moral and practical vision corrected by a view of reality formed by Scripture and by the Christian tradition.

Part of what is at stake in our personal study and meditation on Scripture has to do with the development of a particular way of looking at the world. There is a lot of talk these days about developing a "Christian worldview." Fundamentally, this means developing a particular way of viewing reality, the contours of which are fixed by the story of God as told in Scripture and by principles inherent in the story the Bible tells. Christians believe that Christian faith provides a mental matrix through which we make sense of life and respond to its challenges wisely.

The capacity to distinguish between righteousness and wickedness, between the path of light and the path of darkness, is learned as a person internalizes teachings of the Bible and of wisdom literature and begins to use its principles to evaluate the circumstances of life and possible responses to its challenges. Internalizing wisdom does not eliminate our human need to reason and decide. Wisdom simply gives us the appropriate mental framework needed in order to make good decisions.

In order for a person to properly decide from among various life choices, the teachings of Scripture must be embraced in such a deep way that he or she can focus on the problem at hand. The teachings of Scripture and the example of Christ and of wise people we know and have known become the conscious and unconscious basis for decision-making.[2] As we learn to "indwell" the basic story of the Bible and see the world through a mind formed by it and by others whose personalities reflect its teachings, we are enabled to wisely face the decisions of life.

The notion of "seeing through" a biblical worldview is important. We all see the world through a conceptual grid given to us by

2. Polanyi, *Tacit Dimension*, 17. The sort of teachings we find in wisdom literature guide our decision-making as we interiorize them in such a way that they become a part of the tacit framework we use for moral judgment and action. As we interiorize the teachings of Scripture, we learn to indwell them and evaluate situations, sometimes unconsciously, using them to make concrete decisions. Principles often do not make decisions; they provide a framework in which we evaluate and determine a course of action.

our experiences and what we have learned and internalized through our family, friendships, social interactions, schooling, and the like. Most of the time, we don't think about these presuppositions. They unconsciously shape our view of reality and thereby impact our choices.[3] Unfortunately, the given values of our culture may not lead us to make good choices. Much of the time, they do not. Part of our conversion involves beginning to develop a new way of seeing the world so that we can make truly wise decisions (see Rom 12:1–2). It is only as we develop a wise way of seeing reality that we can act wisely in response to its challenges.

Not long ago, I was called upon to help a person who had badly misjudged a person and a situation. In the process, he injured himself and this family. As the person told me the story of what had happened it became evident that, based upon inaccurate and partial information, his or her mind had developed a completely inaccurate picture of the actual facts. The result was a bad decision. To make good decisions, and especially to make decisions that conform to the will of the Creator, we must have a view of the world and of our place in the world that conforms to the reality of creation and of our place within it.

In our culture, we tacitly accept the importance of material possessions, of good health, of leisure time, pleasure, success, hobbies, and many other things. One of the functions of Scripture is to challenge these assumptions and to substitute other assumptions about what is and is not valuable where our given assumptions are false. The word "conversion" implies that we need a revolution in our thinking by which we see the world in a dramatically different way than we did prior to committing our life to God.

As Christians, we learn to see the world through a different set of glasses than those worn by the majority of the members of our culture. To be a Christian disciple is to perceive and judge the world

3. Michael Polanyi has explored this "tacit dimension" of our perception of the world and understanding in his books *Tacit Dimension* and *Personal Knowledge*.

through a mind formed by the story of Scripture—and particularly that part of Scripture that tells of the life, death, and resurrection of Jesus, who Christians believe was the very Word or Wisdom of God come to dwell among us, so that we can see and understand the wisdom of God embodied in the person of Christ.[4]

The ability to apply wisdom to life is not just a matter of perception. It is also a matter of interiorizing Scripture until it becomes a part of who we are at the core of our being. This is why Proverbs warns believers:

> My child, do not forget my teaching, but let your heart keep my commandments; for length of days and years of life and abundant welfare they will give you. Do not let loyalty and faithfulness forsake you; bind them round your neck, write them on the tablet of your heart. So you will find favour and good repute in the sight of God and of people. Trust in the Lord with all your heart, and do not rely on your own insight. In all your ways acknowledge him, and he will make straight your paths. (3:1–6 NRSV)

Wisdom literature speaks of a wisdom that must be *written on the heart* not just the mind.

The heart is the deepest seat of human motivation. It lies deeper than our conscious perceptions—indeed it shapes them. Our "heart" reflects who we are at the deepest level of our character and motivations. In order to achieve wisdom, the wisdom of God must become who we are at the deepest level of our being. Because this is true, it is important that we interiorize Scripture and the teachings of our faith so that they become a part of our tacit way of viewing the world and how we reach to its challenges. When wisdom is written on our hearts, it works in, through, and beyond our consciousness to impact our decisions in a healthy, helpful way. We will not choose the path of wisdom unless in our hearts we desire that choice.

---

4. Newbigin, *Gospel in a Pluralist Society*, 99.

The Importance of Character

The choice between the path of life and the path of death is not easy, nor is it without its temptations. Character does not develop naturally, nor does it develop necessarily. Character development requires discipline and self-control. Proverbs urges the person learning wisdom not to swerve from the path and to keep one's attention firmly fixed on the goal of living wisely and well (Prov 4:25–27).

The emphasis on self-control brings a modern reader face-to-face with the difference between the way our culture views desires and the way the ancient world viewed desires. People in the modern world are inclined to think of our natural desires as "good" and our satisfaction of those desires as both natural and "good." The authors of biblical wisdom literature, in common with much of the pre-modern world, think of our desires as in need of discipline through reason and self-control. The good person is distinguished both by desiring good things and by the self-discipline to satisfy those desires in a reasonable way.

Such self-control is most obviously demonstrated in the need to avoid and resist temptation—and sexual temptation provides a case in point. The young person must learn to resist and avoid promiscuity. This involves learning self-control, self-discipline, and resistance to desire. Over and over again, Proverbs warns against satisfying desire in an unreasonable and ultimately immoral way. For example, one function of wisdom is to save a young person from the seductive behavior of married people who betray their spouses for momentary pleasure (2:16–18).

The process of developing the kind of character that is guided by a mind formed by Scripture is a slow, step-by-step, "two steps forward, one step back" process. In order for one to form a wise character, there must be a long, slow, patient process of study, confrontation with life-problems, decisions, experiencing results, and reflection. This is why it is virtually impossible for the very young to have a fully developed, wise character. Developing character takes time and practice.

It is our character that determines whether our desires guide us or whether wisdom and reason guide us. Unless there is some check upon our desire for pleasure, for plenty, for possessions, and the like, these desires will unconsciously guide our lives and our decision-making. Ultimately, it is our character that will determine whether we choose the path of life or the path of death.

Questions for Reflection

1. Have you ever been in a situation when you joined a group or organization about which you had some questions, only later to discover that there was something deeply wrong with the group? If so, did you try to remove yourself from the situation?

2. Have you ever embarked on a course of action, only later to discover that the course of action was foolish or wrong? At what point did you make this discovery? What did you do?

3. Can you think of a situation where you made a bad decision and were led into suffering? What happened to your character and reputation as a result?

4. What forms the basis of your decision-making at the deepest level of your being?

Set me as a seal upon your heart, As a seal upon your arm; For love *is as* strong as death, Jealousy *as* cruel as the grave; Its flames *are* flames of fire, A most vehement flame. Many waters cannot quench love, Nor can the floods drown it.

SONG OF SONGS 8:6–7A (NKJV)

Let your fountain be blessed, and rejoice in the wife of your youth, a lovely deer, a graceful doe. Let her breasts fill you at all times with delight; be intoxicated always in her love.

PROVERBS 5:18–19 (ESV)

7

The Faithful Lover

Pride and Prejudice has delighted readers for generations. Author Jane Austin's love story between Elizabeth Bennett and Charles Darcy has formed a part of the moral training of generations of women and men. The saddest characters in the story are Elizabeth's younger sister, Lydia Bennett, and a man who attracts her, Mr. Wickham. Lydia's wild lack of common sense and Mr. Wickham's seductive lack of virtue are compared and contrasted with the character and control of Elizabeth and Mr. Darcy. The novel is one long argument for wisdom and virtue in relationships among the sexes.

In counseling young people about love, the works of Austin are useful. Our capacity for love is a part of the wonder of the human spirit. Animals are sexually motivated for the purpose of the reproduction of the species. Certainly this is the biological basis of human desire. Sexual love is the means by which we are driven to join with another person to propagate our species. This is a basic fact of human biology.

Human love, however, involves more than satisfaction of a biological urge. Throughout human history, people have celebrated the mystery of the bond we call "love." A complete, fully human love involves more than desire for a union that will continue our genes. We are more than animals driven by instinct. Our status as creatures into which the breath of God has been breathed, means that we are spiritual beings. Therefore, human love cannot be merely physical. It involves our minds, our emotions, our imaginations, our consciousness of ourselves and of others around us, and our capacity for choice. Love involves our human capacity to give and to sacrifice for another being.

There is a tendency among some people in our culture to reduce love to sex, as if our higher capacities for love were simply a highly developed expression of sexual desire. The Bible is realistic. Its writers understood that sex is an important aspect of human love. These writers understood the power of desire, just as we do. (One does not need to understand molecular biology to understand that!) The biblical writers also understood that our human capacity for love involves the image of God implanted within our spiritual being. We are not merely very smart animals; we are spiritual and moral beings. If we do not include those aspects of our human character in our love life, we will never experience the fullness of love of which human beings are capable.

The Beauty and Importance of Sexual Love

Does the Bible approve of love, and especially the love of a man and a woman? Is the Bible sexist or misogynist? Does Christian faith involve a denial of the body and repression of natural desires? In order to get a complete picture of what we might call "the wisdom of sex," we must take a look at the fullness of biblical teachings. To do this, we begin with the seldom read book of Song of Songs.

Many people have wondered why Song of Songs was included in our Bible. What motivated the Jews to include a love poem in the canon of Scripture in the first place? Certainly, one reason has to do with the attribution of its writing to King Solomon. However, it is unlikely that ascribing the book to Solomon would have been enough unless the teachings of the book were seen to be somehow important.

Song of Songs is a love poem, or perhaps a collection of love poems, celebrating human love. It is a narrative poem about two lovers. Like all young lovers, they dream of one another, they passionately desire one another, and they speak in touching, almost outlandish terms about the beauty and virtues of the other. They are like young lovers in every age. The girl is no princess from Solomon's court. She is a peasant girl, darkened by the sun (Song 1:6). Her lover thinks that she is the most beautiful woman in all the world with her lovely eyes, full head of hair, flashing teeth, scarlet lips, and shapely figure (4:1–7). For her part, the young girl thinks her shepherd lover is the handsomest man in the world with his skin tanned by the sun, his dark hair, his clear eyes and steady gaze, his strong arms and steady legs. To her, he is altogether the most desirable man in the entire world (5:10–16).

Like lovers everywhere, they dream of one another. The girl dreams of the day he will come to her and hold her in his arms as they make love (3:1). For his part, her lover dreams of the day when he will be able to fondle her—enjoying her lovely breasts (7:6–9). The imagery of the poem is the imagery of two young people intoxicated with romantic love and desire for one another.

Is this all the poem wants to say? Is the poem merely a biblical seduction guide? The answer is found in a little refrain that appears more than once in the poem:

> Daughters of Jerusalem, I charge you by the gazelles and
> by the does of the field: Do not arouse or awaken love until
> it so desires. (3:5)

As the Today's English Version has it, "Promise me, O women of Jerusalem, by the gazelles and wild deer, not to awaken love until the time is right." The Bible invites us to go beyond sentimentality and romanticism to see a deeper reality: sexual love is a wonderful thing, but it is also a dangerous thing and desire must be disciplined until the appropriate time.

In the Judeo-Christian tradition, the right time, the appropriate time for the enjoyment of sex is within the boundaries of marriage, a lifetime commitment of two people to one another. Desire is best controlled until the time is right—until one is prepared to give oneself to another on an unreserved and permanent basis.

The Dangers of Sexual Adventurism

The writers of wisdom literature were generally men, so it is not surprising that biblical warnings center on the dangers of immoral adventuress. If we were to rewrite their encouragement of sexual control and faithfulness, we would rewrite them for both sexes. Today, both genders need the same warning. This cultural difference should not blind us to the essential truth contained in wisdom literature.

A graphic portrayal of the dynamic of temptation is found in the seventh chapter of Proverbs. There, the writer pictures a young man without judgment. One can imagine a nice looking, physically strong, but undisciplined youth. He is walking down the streets of a Middle Eastern city near sundown. Whatever his motivations, he is in the wrong place at the wrong time.

Out from a nearby home comes a woman dressed to attract attention (Prov 7:10). She is loud, and her manner is rebellious. In Middle Eastern culture, where women normally stayed in or near the home and did not very often walk alone in the streets, this woman has a reputation for wanderlust (vv. 11–12). She takes hold of the young man and kisses him, then brazenly invites him into her home (vv. 13–18). This immoral woman entices the young man with the promise of pleasure. The woman is paradigmatic for the unfaithful person who seduces another.

One can easily visualize the young man, confronted by this beautiful, experienced, and available woman. Though filled with desire, he is torn internally, and understands that what he is about to do is wrong. This temptation is perhaps one he might ordinarily have avoided. He can hardly resist this woman. He is tempted and must decide what to do. Finally, he makes his decision: "All at once he followed her like an ox going to the slaughter, like a deer stepping into a noose till an arrow pierces his liver, like a bird darting into a snare, little knowing it will cost him his life" (vv. 22–23). The young man does not know it, but he has made a terrible mistake in going into the home of an adulteress.

Earlier, the voice of the wise father described the dangers of an immoral woman, a seductress who captivates men with her beauty, her speech, and the looks she gives a man (Prov 6:24–25). Falling into the arms of such a woman is likened to scooping up coals and placing them in one's lap or walking on hot coals—a sure fire way to get burned! (vv. 27–28). In the end, a man who falls into such a situation will face the angry response of a husband and disgrace in the community at large. Thus, at the end of this long section of teaching through both advice and story, the author concludes:

> Now then, my sons, listen to me; pay attention to what I say. Do not let your heart turn to her ways or stray into her paths. Many are the victims she has brought down; her slain are a mighty throng. Her house is a highway to the grave, leading down to the chambers of death. (Prov 7:20–27)

In the end, the way of promiscuity is a way of suffering and death.

The Blessing of Sexual Fidelity

Just as wisdom literature makes known the dangers of promiscuity and sexual adventurism, it also promises blessings for those who refrain from promiscuous sexual behavior. This blessing is not just a blessing for future generations, but it is a concrete blessing for each and every individual who chooses fidelity. "One who finds a good spouse finds an excellent thing, and receives favor from the Lord" (18:22; author's paraphrase). The person who rejoices in his or her spouse is the person who receives the greatest blessing.

The Bible teaches that sexual relationships within marriage are a blessing and a joy. Proverbs reads, "Let your fountain be blessed, and rejoice in the wife of your youth, a lovely deer, a graceful doe. Let her breasts fill you at all times with delight; be intoxicated always in her love" (5:18–19 ESV). The love of a stranger is unnecessary for full and complete happiness. Interestingly enough, secular studies confirm that couples who restrict their sexual relationship to marriage are generally happier than those who do not and are also more satisfied in their intimate relationships.

Sexual Wisdom in the Postmodern World

Biblical teaching on sexual morals provides an opportunity to ponder the way the message of wisdom, which originated in a very different culture, can be appropriated today. The culture in which Judeo-Christian teachings originated was patriarchal, at least from a political and economic point of view. In such a culture, much of wisdom teaching was designed for men to warn them about the dangers that can befall a young man in such a culture. Our society is different. Today, women are not typically cloistered in the home. Most women in modern Western culture work outside of the home at least a part of their lives, and all women are typically found outside of the home much of the time. Women have the same rights, freedoms—and temptations—as men.

In our culture, the danger of promiscuity must be seen as applying to men and women alike. Today, both men and women are equally faced with sexual and other temptations, and both need to hear the voice of wisdom warning them to avoid relationships with seducers and seductresses, sexual and otherwise. The context in which the wisdom teaching is given has changed, but the essential truth remains the same. Anyone who has counseled families in which there has been unfaithfulness knows the devastation it brings. Of course, the deceived spouse is filled with anger, resentment, and feelings of betrayal. The children often engage in dangerous behaviors, even if they do not know the facts. Infidelity is a great problem, and seldom brings happiness to those who engage in it. It impacts the participants, their families, their friendships, their friends, and their neighbors. It impacts everyone within the web of their social relationships.

Those who prefer to think this is not true, or who would like to believe that these are words only for an earlier, less sophisticated era, need look no further than the morning paper or the television news for the domestic violence and even murder in which sexual infidelity can result. Cultures change, but human nature does not.

Beyond Sexual Fidelity to Faithfulness

The writers of wisdom literature repeatedly warn against promiscuous behavior. On the surface, this critique has to do with sexual behavior. On a deeper level, however, the critique is about the virtue of faithfulness. Faithfulness in the most intimate relationships of life—and one involving a powerful source of temptation is, among other things, training for faithfulness in all the relationships of life.

Clarissa grew up in a single parent family. Almost immediately after her parent's separation and before the divorce was final, her father moved in with a woman with whom he worked. That relationship lasted for about a year. For another several years, her father "sowed his wild oats" before finally settling down. Clarissa's mother remarried several years later, but only after a couple of stormy relationships that Clarissa observed at close hand. All this left Clarissa wounded, vulnerable, and often promiscuous. Neither of her parents set meaningful boundaries for her behavior. They both were reluctant to express themselves for fear that they would be seen as hypocrites. Now, Clarissa struggles to trust men and wonders what kind of a relationship she will have if she were to marry. She wonders if she would be setting herself up for heartbreak by marrying.

Many years ago, I knew a person who notoriously cheated on his wife. Later, it was revealed that he had also been deceitful with his business associates. Since then, I have had the opportunity to share with young people in business the following adage: "If a man will cheat on his wife, he will cheat on you." Sexual faithfulness within marriage is part of the greater virtue of faithfulness in all of life's relationships. The temptations of sex are great, but in the end no greater than the temptations of greed or lust for power. Proverbs 3 says, "Let love and faithfulness never leave you; bind them around your neck, write them on the tablet of your heart" (v. 3). Faithfulness is ultimately a matter of the heart. It is the capacity to remain true to our deepest commitments and ideals in the midst of temptation to do otherwise. Faithfulness teaches us to value other people, relationships, institutions, and community more than we value our own, transient, and infinitely changeable desires.

The Faithful God

In our human attempts to be faithful, we embrace the faithfulness of the Faithful One, God. The psalmist proclaims, "I will praise you, O Lord, among the nations; I will sing of you among the peoples. For great is your love, reaching to the heavens; your faithfulness reaches to the skies" (Ps 57:9–10). Our human faithfulness is a reflection of God's faithfulness and self-giving love, by which God remains eternally faithful to all creation.[5]

In the New Testament, Jesus is revealed as "faithful and true," the One who is the faithful witness of who God is and of God's plans and purposes for the world, and who in his own divine rule models God's faithfulness for a fallen and broken world (Rev 3:14; 19:11). This faithfulness is and was revealed by his obedient service to God and in his sacrificial death on behalf of the human race (Heb 3:6). Just as Jesus modeled God's self-giving faithfulness, those who follow

---

5. See, for example, Psalms 89:8; 91:4; 98:3; 100:5; 117:2; Isaiah 25:1; 38:19.

Christ should also demonstrate that same kind of faithfulness in all of life (1 Pet 4:19).

When we are faithful to our commitments to those to whom we owe faithfulness, we model the faithfulness of God. In being faithful, we are, in fact, becoming more like God. God has demonstrated his faithfulness to us in the life, death, and resurrection of Jesus Christ. When we are faithful to our families, spouses, children, and others, we bring into this world the faithful love that God is and shares as Father, Son, and Holy Spirit in all eternity.

Questions for Reflection

1. Have you ever experienced the kind of love of which the writer of Song of Songs speaks? What was it like?

2. What are the dangers of a love that is predominately or even entirely sexual passion? Does this kind of love satisfy our deepest needs?

3. What do you see as signs in our society that promiscuous sexual activity is dangerous and can actually harm those who engage in it?

4. In your experience, how does faithfulness in human love draw us closer to God and increase our likeness to God?

He who brings trouble on his family will inherit only wind, and the fool will be servant to the wise.

PROVERBS 11:29

Pay attention to your father, and don't neglect your mother when she grows old. Invest in truth and wisdom, discipline and good sense, and don't part with them. Make your father truly happy by living right and showing sound judgment. Make your parents proud, especially your mother.

PROVERBS 23:22–25 (CEV)

8

Where Wisdom Grows

Wisdom literature assumes that there is a place where wisdom grows first and best—a place that must be created, protected, and treasured. That place is the family. It is within a family that children are conceived, loved, and raised until they achieve adulthood. They will belong to that family when their parents have grown old, and they are the family leaders. The family is not just the place where wisdom is learned. It is the first and primary place where it is practiced.

Prohibitions against promiscuous sexual behavior in wisdom literature are part of a greater objective: the protection of the family as a place of wisdom, love, economic security, and intergenerational nurture and care. The writers of the Old Testament believed that they were part of a large, extended family: the children of Abraham, Isaac, and Jacob. That family was fundamental to their view of the world and how they ought to live. For them, the family was not just the fundamental unit of their society; it was their society. This may explain why the writers of wisdom literature do not so much teach about the family and its importance as they assume the centrality and value of family life. We, unfortunately, live in a much different culture.

Wendy and her brother Paul are growing up in a blended family. Their mother, Abigail, was married before, and they are children of that marriage. Wendy's stepfather, Roy, has two children by a prior marriage. They live with Roy and Abigail about half the time. Roy and Abigail also have a child, Beverly, who is five. Their marriage is a happy one, but the pressure of raising teenagers combined with their strong sense that they do not want Beverly to suffer the same sense of dislocation that the other children experienced often leaves Wendy and her brother feeling that they do not belong. Their birth father, Sam, remarried several years ago, and then divorced again. This has left Wendy and Paul suspicious of their biological father. The family feels economic pressures. Sam only occasionally pays child support. Therefore, Abigail must work. The family spends little time together except on the weekends. Often, the weekends are spent doing household chores and taking children to various athletic events. There is little time to just be a family.

Families Where Wisdom Grew

Ancient Israel was an agrarian society. Most people directly or indirectly worked the land, which was the primary source of wealth. As in most primitive societies, family units consisted of multiple generations living under one roof and working together in the family business. In such a culture, the family was not just a fundamental unit for bearing and raising children, it was also the fundamental economic unit of society.

The majority of children grew up working the land. A few people were employed in trades such as carpentry or in commercial businesses. In time, children became a part of the family economy. Later, as the parents became too old to work, the children would take over the family work and provide for the parents while training and preparing their own children to take over responsibility to provide for the care of the extended family.

Israel consisted of a series of geographic areas in which one tribe was dominant (i.e., Judah or Dan or Benjamin). In an agrarian culture with limited means of transportation, most people spent their lives within a limited geographic area. Most were born, reared, married, raised families, grew old, and died within the boundaries of their tribal homeland. Cities were small by modern standards. Even those who lived in cities, villages, and little towns rarely traveled except for traders who traveled in caravans. In such a culture, family and relatives were the center of life and loyalties.

The structure of society also reinforced the structure of the family. Ancient Israel, within which wisdom literature grew, was what we would call "patriarchal." Within such cultures a woman left her family of origin and lived in the household of her husband. When more than one generation lived in a home, the oldest living male in the household was the head of the household, and each husband was responsible for his wife and children.

With many adults living in close proximity and relationship with one another, the Jews developed detailed sexual codes prohibiting a male from "uncovering the nakedness" of close relatives—the wives of one's father or brothers, sisters, and their children, and other family members who commonly lived within the household (Lev 18:1–19; 20:10–21).[6] These codes and the other restrictions on sexual behavior reflect the experience of the Jewish people as they reflected upon the problems of social life within the communities with which they were familiar.

Women seldom left the vicinity of the household. Indeed it was the mark of a sexually loose woman that she traveled beyond the socially acceptable geographic boundaries of family life. Although women lived in a patriarchal society, the Bible reflects a reality that is more complicated than most modern people recognize. Women

---

6. For an extended series of essays concerning the structure and nature of Jewish families in ancient Israel, see Perdue et al., *Families in Ancient Israel*.

were not as helpless as some commentators imagine. Women had legal and social rights. For example, divorce was regulated in order to secure the rights of the weaker party (Deut 22:13–19; 24:1–4). And within the family unit, wives had an important role.

Proverbs 31 eloquently speaks of the honor due to a wife who diligently managed her household. The wife was in charge of feeding and clothing the family and providing for their basic needs. Educationally, the wife commonly provided for the earliest education and discipline of her children and for all the education of her daughters until they were ready to marry and enter the home of their husband.

If the eldest male was at the head of the household, and each father was the head of his wife, the children of the household were the youngest, least independent, and most vulnerable members of the family unit. However, children were not unimportant. They were the future of the family, the security of the parents as they grew old, and the fruit of the love of the parents. The story of Abraham arises out of the importance that Abraham attaches to having an heir, and the stories of Isaac and Jacob reinforce the importance of children to the patriarchs.

Parents, grandparents, aunts, and uncles, and trusted servants who lived within the household, were in constant contact with children of both genders. Families lived on farms or in small cities, villages, or townships, many of which were so small as to be primarily made up of the extended family. Other well-known individuals watched over and protected children, passed on knowledge, and served as examples for growing children. In such a society, the accumulated wisdom (and prejudices) of the family, tribe, and nation were passed on to children informally from their earliest days. This intergenerational wisdom was both practical—how to conduct the family's affairs—and moral—standards of behavior expected of children and adults. The basic pattern of existence was both stable and successful for the passing on of information required for a young person to grow into a successful adult.

A Culture in Which Wisdom Is Lost

Scholars are almost unanimous in their evaluation of the American family: the family unit is extraordinarily weak. If in ancient Israel families lived in large, intergenerational groupings, today the basic family unit consists of a mother, father, and children. Many children in America will spend at least a part of their lives in a family unit lacking one of their biological parents. An increasing number of children may live with neither of their biological parents but with grandparents or other relatives. Grandparents seldom occupy the same home as their grandchildren, and many live a long distance away and seldom see their grandchildren. Children are not regularly exposed to the wisdom of the eldest and most experienced members of the family. This is a great loss to children and grandchildren, as well as to the elderly.

In the ancient world, and really until relatively late in the modern era, most children grew up in what we would call rural communities, where people lived in close proximity to their work. In this kind of a culture, families worked, ate, and slept near one another, even if grandparents lived in a separate home. Today, most adults commute to work in offices and businesses in which children are not able to be present. Most working parents leave the home early in the morning and do not return until evening. Constant interaction and intergenerational training in practical and moral skills is not possible in such an environment.

Modern culture is characterized by excessive individualism with the result that families are increasingly fragile as some couples place personal self-fulfillment above the interests of their children. While many American children spend part of their formative years without at least one of their parents in the household, the remaining parent is often preoccupied with providing for the household. Since all of the housework and at least some of the monetary requirements of the household must now be met by a single person, the single parent household, by its very nature, provides less nurture and less security than a dual parent household.

Whichever parent is absent, the unique contribution of the missing parent to the household is also missing. In many cases, it is the father who is absent, which has unfortunate effects on both boys and girls. If and when the parents remarry, the new adult in the household is not the biological parent of the child, and therefore, often lacks an intuitive understanding of the child—and may lack any interest at all.

The causes of the problems American marriages face are many and complex. They include a separation of sexual relationships, marriage, and parenthood; a shift in the ideal of marriage from a lifelong commitment to children and the household to so-called "soul mate marriages," as well as the emergence of several forms of what might be called "quasi-marital" forms of community. We also see a general decline of involvement by fathers in the lives of their children, and perhaps most importantly, a change in the focus of the meaning and purpose of adulthood from traditional concerns of marriage and family to work, hobbies, and other activities.[7]

The decline of family life has had a definite impact on both children and parents. Children suffer from a lack of meaningful connection with parents. An absent parent cannot bond with and mentor a child, preparing them for adulthood. Children who grow up in isolated circumstances may suffer lasting emotional damage, including relational disorders, fear of failure, and difficulty in managing situations involving conflict.[8] Parents increasingly suffer from the stress of coordinating families in which there is not a reliable center to family life. They struggle to do the best thing by their children in circumstances where it is difficult to discern what the right thing might be.

Some years ago, I had the opportunity to spend several days with two fine young people of our congregation. Both were children of fine parents who experienced divorce. I had the opportunity to hear them tell of the difficulties they had as children reconciling the

7. B. Whitehead and Popenoe, "State of Our Unions," 1–8.
8. Ibid., 5–6.

demands of parents who lived in separate households. Little things were often problematic, like a textbook left behind at the wrong house, resulting in either a missed homework assignment or a late night trip across the city. Both mentioned the stress of holidays with both parents desiring and expecting attention.

At the same time, single parents often complain that they have difficulty establishing reasonable boundaries for their children because of the constant bidding for affection by an ex-spouse, the stress of being unable to discipline when needed for fear of alienating a child (who may then prefer to live with the other parent), and the constant jockeying of the demands of multiple family schedules. Whatever the necessity of the divorce, there are consequences to the children, consequences that can include a deep insecurity and lack of self-worth.

This description of divorce and its costs is not meant to shame the many, many divorced and remarried couples that are diligently trying to raise and provide a home for their children while sometimes also caring for aging parents too. Every pastor knows many of them—and admires what they are doing. Like it or not, for many years our society is likely to be characterized by family instability. Blended or not, families are generally not as strong as in former generations. Many people need the loving help of family, friends, neighbors, and congregations to provide assistance in raising their children. This is one of the most important ministries of our day and time. At the same time, the help churches can give to broken families will never supply the benefits of growing up in a secure, loving family surrounded by parents, grandparents, and others.

Recovering the Family as Central to Civilization

Proverbs teaches that "Like a bird that strays from its nest is one who strays from home" (27:8 NRSV). A nest is a place of safety and of nurture. To wander from the nest is to be in danger of being lost, attacked, or taken away from a place of safety and protection. Our society is full of men and women who have strayed from their nest and now wander in search of stability, meaning, family, and a structure for life. Unfortunately, their children also face the same loss of stability, meaning, structure, and place—and especially the nest we call "home." Those of us who inhabit a restless culture characterized by a loss of family ties can profit from considering the consequences of diminished family life. In fact, one might say that our culture is in the late stages of a vast and unsuccessful experiment in ignoring the importance of family life. We need to recover the notion of family as central to social life and social stability.

In recent years many social analysts have suggested, and some societal leaders have encouraged, a return to some sense of communal responsibility for children, which would inevitably involve some sense that societal wisdom must be passed along to children. When former First Lady, Senator, and Secretary of State Hillary Clinton wrote her book *It Takes a Village,* many commentators criticized or made fun of the title. Whatever the intentions of the author, the book embodies a truth: it *does* take a family and a caring community to provide children with a stable environment in which they can acquire the skills and character they need to face the problems of life. Parents and families must be a part of a larger culture of support for children.

Within wider society, families play the central role in the raising and support of children. It is within families that children first learn the virtues of cooperation, reasonable obedience to authority, deference to experience, hard work, and a host of other virtues. These virtues will not be available to the larger community unless they are first learned within the home and family. This is not to suggest that family life should be considered a mere duty. The writers of wisdom literature understood the problems and temptations of family life, but they also understood its pleasures. In the modern and postmodern world, we have sometimes focused on the problems and temptations of family life and devalued its joys and pleasures. In the process, we have forgotten the importance of belonging to a family that will love, understand, and support its members in all the challenges and difficulties of life.

To say that family life is important and central to human happiness is not to defend a kind of family life that damages children and spouses. Such families need to be identified and helped to overcome their brokenness. Members of dysfunctional families that cannot be helped must be assisted in other ways. This is one of the central roles of the church and other organs of society.

Every pastor, social worker, or other caring professional sees the results of the weakness of Western families: children growing up with only their peers and television and media to guide them, wounded adults who love their children but are unable to find ways to show that love in healthy ways, young adults trying to form families without the assistance of parents and grandparents, and grandparents and older people facing the end of life alone.

The excessive move toward individualism breeds a society in which children often lack the kind of close emotional intimacy with their parents that allows them to develop into healthy, well-balanced people. Too often, parents are emotionally absent from children as they seek business success, affluence, personal satisfaction, and personal pleasure. It is possible that the individualism of our culture is a reaction to the excessive communitarian nature of pre-modern societies. What is needed is a balanced recovery of the importance of extended family and community within the lives of our children. This may be especially true in America where families and communities have become almost pathologically weak during the past century.

In the West, we need to recover the value of traditional family life. We can see in many movies a kind of longing for the values found in a pre-modern, pre-industrial society. I recently watched a movie called *Come Live with Me* starring Jimmy Stewart and Hedy Lamarr. The movie is a romantic comedy about Bill Smith, a struggling writer, and Johnny Jones, a showgirl who is having an affair with a married man. At the beginning of the movie, the Department of Immigration advises Johnny that she will be deported because her temporary passport has expired. Only if Johnny marries can she remain in the United States. That evening, Johnny runs into Bill and explains that she needs to marry an American citizen within a week. Since Bill is broke, she agrees to pay him $17.80 a week in exchange for temporarily marrying her. Two months later, Bill is writing a book and falling deeply in love with Johnny. Meanwhile, Johnny continues her affair with the married man. Finally, Bill coerces Johnny to go on a trip with him to see his grandmother who lives in the country. When Bill and Johnny arrive, Bill's grandmother is needle pointing a sampler with a piece of advice about "time healing all wounds." During the meeting between Johnny and Bill's grandmother, there is the following exchange:

> Grandma: After all, time does heal all wounds.
>
> Johnny Jones: Does it?
>
> Grandma: No arguing about it. There's no arguing with any of the old sayings because that's why they are old 'cause they tell the truth, and the truth lasts.[9]

Come Live with Me is ultimately about family, the wisdom of older people, and the values of traditional life as compared to the shallow and false values of the city and of the "smart people." The scene between Johnny and Grandma reflects the desire of contemporary people for the security and stability of traditional families and their strength, wisdom, and values. Unfortunately, we have not been able to find ways of meeting the need expressed by that desire.

There is probably no aspect of contemporary culture more in need of rethinking than the attitude of the media and others towards family life. When people, young and old, need help, families are the crucial first caregivers. The sense of isolation so many contemporary young people feel partially stems from weak and distant family life. Human beings were simply not meant to live in isolation—and especially not in isolation from the fundamental social unit of the family.

---

9. *Come Live with Me*, MGM, 1941.

Questions for Reflection

1. How important was your family in your own life and in your development as a human being? Did your parents pass on wisdom and principles for living? If so, how? If not, what were the results?

2. If you were to make one change in your family based on this chapter, what would it be?

3. What are some concrete steps you could take to make your family a place where love is felt and wisdom grows?

4. If you are a member of a church, what things could your church do to assist families in becoming a true training ground for life?

Treasures gained by wickedness do not profit, but righteousness delivers from death. The Lord does not let the righteous go hungry, but he thwarts the craving of the wicked. A slack hand causes poverty, but the hand of the diligent makes rich. A son who gathers in summer is prudent, but a son who sleeps in harvest brings shame.

PROVERBS 10:2–5 (RSV)

9

The Life of Self-Control

Every parent, sooner or later, asks a child to stop crying and hears in response, "I can't." The parent, of course, knows that the child "can" in the sense that the child has the capacity for self-control. Most parents learn (after a child or two) that small children actually feel they do not have the ability to exercise self-control. We even begin to find charming their lack of understanding. What is stressful but charming in small children is not charming in teenagers and adults. Too often in our culture people lack basic wisdom and self-control. Worse, we meet those who think human beings cannot effectively exercise self-control—or don't need to exercise self-control.

The ancient world understood that virtue requires self-control. It is not something with which a person is born; it is something a person achieves. It demands discipline and practice. We live in an age inclined to think of people as naturally good and naturally able to achieve good character if only they are raised properly and have the right kind of schooling. For us, the "good" and the "natural" are often confused. We regard it as virtuous when people follow their natural instincts and less than virtuous if they resist them. We do not think of parents and teachers as responsible to train children in virtue so much as we consider parents and others responsible to channel natural impulses in ways that are not harmful to society and other people. Modern people often subconsciously believe that morality can ultimately be reduced to biology. As we will see, this view is inadequate to the complexity of the human person.

Randi is a young person in her late twenties. She grew up in a Christian home, but in college she drifted from her faith. Yet she thinks of herself as a spiritual person and a good person. Recently, she was subpoenaed before a Grand Jury concerning a business transaction in which her employer was involved. Although she was not directly involved, as she gave her testimony, she realized for the first time that part of her duties made possible a situation in which many people were hurt. It made her wonder about herself and her character. Often she thinks to herself, "Perhaps I am not the person I thought I was."

The word "virtue" has a root meaning of "excellence." In moral discourse, the Greek word "arête" meant attaining a certain kind of moral character or moral excellence.[1] Excellence of character is not something we are born with and naturally develop. It is something we attain by a life of discipline and self-control. Human beings are capable of moral excellence, but it will not develop without work. Therefore, the ancients would have disagreed with the notion that virtue "comes naturally" in the modern sense. To them, the virtuous life involved disciplining and channeling natural impulses. Children and adults had to be trained in virtue. The most important part of that training was designed to make the young person desire the virtuous life. This was often accomplished by the telling of stories and legends.[2] They understood that people are born with different innate characteristics, some of which make virtue harder to attain than others. Yet, they also believed that everyone, whatever their natural endowments, needed to undergo training and discipline to achieve

1. Kittel and Friedrich, "Arête," 77.
2. A modern attempt at this kind of moral training is found in Bennett, *Book of Virtues*.

noble character. This is why Proverbs begins by teaching that sayings of wisdom are profitable for discipline (1:2).

The kind of training virtue requires is not just needed in children. The life of virtue is something that a person continues to work on throughout all of life. This is why wisdom literature teaches that wisdom is

> for attaining wisdom and discipline; for understanding words of insight; for acquiring a disciplined and prudent life, doing what is right and just and fair; for giving prudence to the simple, knowledge and discretion to the young—let the wise listen and add to their learning, and let the discerning get guidance—for understanding proverbs and parables, the sayings and riddles of the wise. (vv. 2–6)

For the writers of wisdom literature, there is no part of life—youth, midlife, or old age—where the need for growth in virtue is not necessary.

The virtuous life is a lifelong marathon. Although there may be special training in technique and the like when one is young or just beginning, each race requires the discipline of training. The training may change and evolve as one grows older, but it never stops. The life of wisdom is a lifelong effort of thought, training, action, and reflection.

The Meaning of the Virtuous Life

What do we mean when we talk about the need for the virtuous life? The word "virtue" in its most general usage refers to the ability of a person or thing to accomplish the purpose for which it was created or made. In ordinary language, we speak of a thing as having virtue if it is well made, performs its function, and lasts a long time. Something that accomplishes the purpose for which it was created is virtuous in this sense. This notion carries over to the human usage of the term. Historically, men were virtuous if they were strong and courageous, and able to work in the field and defend their families. Women were virtuous if they were chaste and ladylike, able also to do the work of the home and provide for the welfare of their families. The exact nature of virtue differed among cultures and civilizations, but the idea that virtue is related to success in the business of life is common to all ideas of virtue.

One development of the late modern and postmodern world has been a realization that not all cultures and civilizations agree on the precise qualities of a virtuous life. We call this understanding "cultural relativism." The ancient Greeks thought a kind of manliness and courage in battle, ending in a courageous death involved the highest form of virtue—hence the fate of Achilles in Homer's Iliad. In nineteenth-century America, the young person who went from rags to riches through hard work, intelligence, and grit embodied the quintessence of the virtuous life. So the question arises, "How are we to coordinate different notions of the end of human life?" Are we to simply say they are equivalent and no decision can be made between them?

There is no question but that among the world's religions there is a lack of agreement about the fundamental qualities of a virtuous person. In the modern world we experience different ideas about what constitutes success in life. Is the virtuous person the rugged individualist who attains success over all odds? Is the virtuous person one who escapes the pain of desire by achieving Nirvana like the Buddha? Is the virtuous person one who endures privation and suffering for the good of others, like Mother Teresa? Is the virtuous person one who fights a holy war as a few radical Muslims believe? Is the virtuous person one who self-actualizes his or her own subjective choices as modern secular people sometimes believe?

To some degree these kind of questions take us to the deepest question plaguing the modern world: "Is there any real core nature to our humanity—a core nature that enables us to speak of a kind of virtue that is truly cross cultural and that all human beings ought to seek to achieve?" "Is it possible to choose rationally among ethical systems and notions of the good life?" The traditional Judeo-Christian answer to this question is "Yes." Christians believe that all human beings have a core image of God imbedded within them (Gen 1:27). This image may be distorted by sin and by self-centered selfishness, but it is there and should be respected and nurtured. Scholars have differing ideas about what this "image of God" involves, but there are certainly features of human beings that are unique.

Human beings are capable of being rational. We are self-conscious—aware of our separate identity and understanding of nature and others. We are able not just to understand and react to situations, but we can reflect upon life and upon our responses to situations. We are self-critical, able to ask the question, "Could I have done better?" While the role of instinct remains important for human existence, our sense of self and our rational power of decision mean that we can reflect upon and direct our natural impulses. One common feature of the virtuous person is that he or she has learned to guide their natural impulses according to reason.

Human beings appear to be the only creatures able to understand and appreciate the interrelated, rationality of the world God created. We have developed the natural sciences as ways to exercise that capacity. We are creative. We have imagination. This means that we are not only able to conceive of the world the way it is, we are also able to consider that the world might be otherwise. Art, music, and the literary sciences reflect our capacity for imagination. Finally, we are moral beings. We instinctively consider some actions by others and ourselves to be fair or unfair.

Every parent has experienced this innate concept of fairness the first time a child says: "That is not fair!" When I was young, I took advantage of my younger brother by trading him nickels (which were larger and seemingly more valuable) for dimes. When he learned the truth, he immediately accused me of being unfair. My mother agreed and asked me to give him his money back. Interestingly, I immediately knew they were right. Human moral abilities allow us to delight in things and actions we consider good, beautiful, or wise.

This innate sense of fairness is there, but it can be lost, and so must be developed to control behavior.

The Torah of the Old Testament and the law of love given by Jesus in the New Testament are descriptions of a kind of life lived according to the nature God implanted within human beings. "Thou shalt not kill," the foundation of the biblical virtue of peaceableness, and "Thou shalt not commit adultery," the foundation of the biblical virtue of faithfulness, are not seen by the biblical writers as simply laws we must follow because they were given by a divine lawgiver. They are expressions of what it means to live in the image of a God of steadfast love. They are part of the nature of things—a nature that we cannot ignore without distorting that image of God within us.

What are the core virtues that, according to wisdom literature, enable human beings to live wisely and achieve the virtue for which they were created?[3] Is it possible to identify in wisdom teachings a core group of virtues that characterize the virtuous life? Throughout history, there have been attempts to list them. The Greeks considered four virtues, justice (equity), wisdom (prudence), courage (fortitude), and moderation (self-control) to be fundamental or "natural" virtues. The virtuous person concentrated on developing these virtues because they were fundamental to all other virtues. In the Roman Catholic theology, these four natural virtues were supplemented by three theological (or spiritual) virtues: faith, hope, and love.

Many attempts have been made to find an intellectual basis for the natural and supernatural virtues. Wisdom literature is one of the primary places to which people look when they undertake this task, and there are many places where justice, wisdom, courage, and moderation are urged. However, all of these attempts involve a kind of reductionism. Wisdom literature is far too complex to be reduced to a single formula or set of virtues. So this chapter simply outlines

3. A warning is important here. One of the mistakes of modernity has been its tendency to "reductionism." In the case of wise living, there is a tendency to reduce the plurality and complexity of wisdom and the wise life to a set of virtues. The discussion that follows is for the purpose of increasing understanding, not as a theoretical reduction.

thematic virtues that are urged upon us over and over again in biblical wisdom literature.

The Life of Humble Faith

As previously noted, it is not without reason that Proverbs begins with the injunction, "The fear of the LORD is the beginning of knowledge, but fools despise wisdom and discipline" (1:7). Later it is put in this way, "The fear of the LORD is the beginning of wisdom, and knowledge of the Holy One is understanding" (9:10). The notion that the wise life begins with understanding God as the source of meaning, wisdom, and purpose in life is fundamental to Judeo-Christian understanding. There is no virtue without faith in the God who created us and who implanted within us his image. Once we have God in the right place, humans find their place, a place of humility as a created being who is fragile, fallible, finite, and fallen.

We have already noted that the word "fear" is best translated, "deep reverence." Why is reverence for God essential to achieving virtue in the eyes of the Judeo-Christian tradition? By recognizing that there is a God and an order implanted in the universe to which we must conform, human beings begin to develop a supremely important virtue—humility. When we become humble, we understand the inevitability of errors and mistakes in judgment, the complexity of life and of people, and above all the need to act with care and to suspend judgment about people and things. Without a sense of human limits, it is impossible to achieve the kind of virtuous life that God desires.

Humility is the parent of many virtues. It is humility that enables us to see ourselves, our ideas, and our plans as potentially flawed and in need of revision. It is humility that allows us to accept that others are flawed as we are flawed, so that tolerance of behavior and opinions with which we disagree becomes possible. Most importantly, humility causes us to realize how little we know, that our knowledge of people, situations, and events is partial and imperfect. From this humility, we develop the deep desire to know more, understand more, and tolerate disagreement and different understandings. Paradoxically, coming to recognize our human limitations is central to overcoming them. As we recognize the extent of our ignorance and fallibility, we have taken the most important step in overcoming them and making progress.

The Life of Peaceable Honesty

After Proverbs introduces the importance of humble faith, it goes on to teach:

> My child, if sinners entice you, do not consent. If they say, "Come with us, let us lie in wait for blood; let us wantonly ambush the innocent; like Sheol let us swallow them alive and whole, like those who go down to the Pit. We shall find all kinds of costly things; we shall fill our houses with booty. Throw in your lot among us; we will all have one purse"—my child, do not walk in their way, keep your foot from their paths; for their feet run to evil, and they hurry to shed blood. For in vain is the net baited while the bird is looking on; yet they lie in wait—to kill themselves! and set an ambush—for their own lives! (1:10–18 NRSV)

A second characteristic of the wise life might be called "non-violent honesty."

The Jews were not a warlike people. Abraham and the patriarchs were Bedouins traveling though regions controlled by sovereigns who were more powerful and often violent.[4] Frequently, they camped near towns and cities in which there were more inhabitants than their tribe included. In such a situation, avoiding conflict was as important a virtue as the ability to respond to violence when necessary.

---

4. The travels of Abraham, the father of Israel, are illustrative of this virtue. Abraham can respond with force when necessary, as he proves in his response to the abduction of Lot (Gen 14). Yet he is willing to deceive Pharaoh concerning Sarah's relationship with him to avoid violence (Gen 12:10–20).

Proverbs begins with a warning against violence to achieve economic ends, and that warning includes urging non-violence in the conduct of all economic and personal affairs (see Prov 1:10–16). Armed robbery is forbidden. The Sixth Commandment, "Thou shalt not kill" (Exod 20:13) is but a specific instance of a broader notion contained in the Torah and the New Testament: violence is a distortion of God's intention for humanity. God's intention is peaceable relatedness. Therefore, violence in the attainment of economic, personal, or even public ends is to be avoided. There may be instances where violence is necessary, and the Bible records many such instances. However, violence is never the best result in any situation. Violence and evil go together, and the person who comes to rely on violence inevitably commits some evil. Wisdom, therefore, urges young people to avoid dishonest people because they are constantly devising violent and corrupt schemes (Prov 24:1–2).

If peaceableness is a virtue in the writings of the wise men, it is connected with another virtue: honesty. So wisdom teaches that, "Truthful lips endure forever, but a lying tongue lasts only a moment" (12:19). Honesty in speech may not always result in riches, but the honest person who is poor is better off than a dishonest person who attains wealth (19:1). Honesty in words is not enough. A wise and virtuous person must necessarily be honest in his or her dealings with others.

Honesty is not just a personal virtue. It is also a socio-economic virtue. In the ancient world many transactions were conducted on the basis of weights and scales. It was a common practice for the seller to misrepresent the quantity of goods being sold by under weighing them. Wisdom, therefore, teaches that, "Diverse weights are an abomination to the Lord, and false scales are not good" (20:23 RSV). Practices that involve economic dishonesty are ultimately against the will of God—and, therefore, against the entire grain of the universe and our created nature. An honest person gets a day's wage for a day's work and gives a day's work for a day's wage. In dealing with others, an honest person gives the other full credit for what has been bought or sold. The frequent specific injunctions against commercial dishonesty are a part of a bigger ethical encouragement to be honest in all dealings with other people, personal and economic.

Not so long ago, I was reading in a financial publication about a financial transaction in which one customer of an investment bank came to the bank asking that it create a pool of mortgages of the lowest possible quality. That customer wanted to "short" (or bet on a decline in value of) those pooled mortgages. The investment bank did as requested and then sold the mortgages to others without fully and completely disclosing either the impetus behind the transaction or that the investment bank itself had shorted the mortgages as had its original customer.[5] Surprisingly, many commentators on the article found nothing questionable in what the bank had done, despite enormous losses to customers, some undoubtedly retired, widowed, or participating in one of the many institutional accounts to which these mortgages were sold. This is only one of many examples of how we have come to assume that fair dealing is unnecessary in a world dominated by a kind of Darwinian notion of free enterprise in which there are no rules for economic life except "buyer beware." This is not the notion of the Bible or of wisdom literature.

We are all constantly tempted to make our lives easier by acts of dishonesty, great or small. The practice of underpaying taxes is but one common example. The wise person resists this temptation. This does not mean we must say all that we know or not be shrewd in financial dealings. It means we must be honest and straightforward in our dealings with others. Honesty is not just a personal virtue, it is a social virtue that is necessary for a person or a society to be successful.

The Life of Sober Judgment

Wisdom literature constantly encourages readers to develop insight into people and situations, as well as the judgment to act on that

5. Story and Morgenson, "S.E.C. Accuses Goldman of Fraud."

insight. Therefore, the Bible discourages behaviors that inhibit one's ability to judge wisely. This means that sobriety is an essential part of the wise life. Right at the beginning of this discussion, it is important to point out that the wisdom literature does not teach a kind of narrow, life-denying, puritanical approach to the subject of drinking. Jesus, the Word Made Flesh, was criticized for drinking by those who thought that a holy person should not (Luke 7:34–36). In response to their criticism, Jesus responded with one of his many wisdom sayings:

> But to what shall I compare this generation? It is like children sitting in the marketplaces and calling to their playmates, "We played the flute for you, and you did not dance; we sang a dirge, and you did not mourn." For John came neither eating nor drinking, and they say, "He has a demon." The Son of Man came eating and drinking, and they say, "Look at him! A glutton and a drunkard, a friend of tax collectors and sinners!" Yet wisdom is justified by her deeds. (Matt 11:16–19 ESV)

There were and are many who think that faithful people should embrace an extreme kind of self-restraint exhibited by those who had taken Nasserite vows (which prohibited drinking anything alcoholic) as practiced by some of the extreme sects of the Judaism of Jesus' day. As healthy as this may be for some, it is not absolutely required of all Christians by any fair reading of Scripture. The proof of wisdom is in the practical results, the "deeds" of the wise person, not in an abstract, life denying morality. There is no question but that habitual drunkenness (and by extension the modern habit of using recreational drugs) is both harmful and destructive of wise behavior, so the wise person is not led astray by the love of alcohol. "Wine is a mocker, strong drink a brawler; and whoever is led astray by it is not wise" (Prov 20:1). The key in this area as in so many others is a wise and moderate exercise of self-control.

A wise person not only avoids excessive drinking, but also avoids being around those who are constantly feeding their human desire for food and drink. Therefore, the wisdom writers taught:

> Listen, my child, and be wise. Keep your mind on what is right. Don't drink too much wine or eat too much food. Those who drink and eat too much become poor. They sleep too much and end up wearing rags. (23:19–21 NCV)

Wisdom is indeed justified by its results, and the general result of habitual drunkenness is poor judgment.

Life is a series of decisions, and the wise person is ready to make decisions when and where the necessity to make them arises. Leaders and those in authority, who are constantly called upon to make decisions, are especially warned about the dangers of drinking: "It is not for kings to drink wine, not for rulers to crave beer, lest they drink and forget what has been decreed, and deprive all the oppressed of their rights" (Prov 31:4–5). One major disadvantage of excessive drinking and/or the use of mind-altering drugs is that they make one forget the teachings of wisdom. This loss of control involves the constant danger of some kind of misbehavior or mistaken decision that will injure themselves and others.

Sobriety is not a virtue that exists for its own sake, like love for others. It is a virtue that exists for the sake of a deeper virtue: the ability to make good decisions. In fact, sobriety can require that we change personality characteristics, such as impulsiveness, which impair our ability to make wise decisions. Wisdom cannot be attained without constant attention to people and situations. This constant attention results in what the Bible calls "insight"—the ability to see into the interior meaning of a person or a situation, to understand the complexity of people and their motivations. Insight requires sober judgment and avoiding habits that might impair it.

The Life of Diplomatic Communication

Wisdom literature constantly addresses the power of words and the importance of wise communication. A characteristic of the fool and worthless person is habitual perversion of speech:

> A worthless person, a wicked man, goes about with crooked speech, winks with his eyes, signals with his feet, points with his finger, with perverted heart devises evil, continually sowing discord; therefore calamity will come upon him suddenly; in a moment he will be broken beyond healing. (6:12–15 ESV)

Perverse, low, or angry speech leads to suffering, poor social relationships, and failure.

A close reading of wisdom literature discloses many ways in which human speech can be self-defeating. Harshness stirs up opposition (Prov 15:1). Words designed to stir up trouble end up creating trouble for the one who speaks them (10:14). Rash words hurt others unnecessarily (12:18). Too many words let others know how little we actually understand (12:23). Quarreling is never a good idea (17:14; 26:21; 29:11). Meddling in the quarrels of others is a big mistake (26:17).

On the other hand, wise speech blesses a person: "From a wise mind comes wise speech; the words of the wise are persuasive. Kind words are like honey—sweet to the soul and healthy for the body" (16:23–24 NLT). It turns out that the destiny of a person is largely dependent upon the ability to control the tongue, speak wisely, and avoid perversion in speech. Wise speech brings a blessing, but foolish speaking brings suffering and failure.

A wise person is often silent and careful not to talk too much (Prov 10:14; 12:23; 29:20). A wise person thinks before he or she speaks and weighs carefully what is said (15:28; 17:27–28; 18:13). Whenever possible, a wise person does not belittle others or disclose secrets (11:12–13). A wise person uses his or her speech to avoid conflict, pour oil on the waters of potential bad feelings, and create good feelings in others (15:4; 16:23–24; 17:14). Self-control in speech is one very good way to stay out of trouble and succeed in life (21:23–24).

Jesus teaches that it is not what is outside of us that sullies us, but what is inside of us and comes out in our words:

> What comes out of a person is what defiles them. For it is from within, out of a person's heart, that evil thoughts come—sexual immorality, theft, murder, adultery, greed, malice, deceit, lewdness, envy, slander, arrogance and folly. All these evils come from inside and defile a person. (Mark 7:20–23)

Our deeds come out of who we are and further define us. Most often who we are is shown by our words. If I am arrogant, foolish, a slanderer, a gossip, or whatever, my words disclose this to the world. A wise person monitors his or her speech, for in monitoring our speech, we monitor who we are and who we are becoming. Our speech is important because our speech reveals our character.

When my wife and I were engaged to be married, we went to a wise older pastor for counsel. His counseling technique was a bit old fashioned, but his advice has turned out to be true. He began by quoting the New Testament book of James and its teaching that the tongue is a blazing fire (Jas 3:6). Then, he made an observation: in his fifty years as a pastor he never counseled a couple involved in a divorce in which words that should have never been said did not form a part of the marital problem. Over thirty years of marriage and twenty-plus years of ministry confirm his observation. Our speech impacts our relationships, and our relationships impact who we are and what we become.

The wise person is especially careful about words. The word "communication" comes from the same Latin root as the word "communion." Communication is the most powerful way in which we enter into communion with the lives of others. Proper communication is always communication in the image of the One who is the source and ground of all communion among human beings. Since the nature of that person is self-giving love, so our communication with others ought always to be grounded in that kind of unselfish love. This is why self-controlled, loving speech was also a concern of the New Testament writers (Col 4:6; 1 Cor 13:5; Jas 3). If Jesus came to proclaim and embody the kingdom of God and the peace God intends for the entire world, and if we are the ambassadors of that kingdom, there is nothing more important than the way we speak and embody the divine love of Christ.

The Life of Generous and Just Concern for Others

Over and over again, wisdom literature reveals that a virtuous and wise person is characterized by a just concern for others. A virtuous person is not just concerned for him or herself and his or her family and close acquaintances. The virtuous life takes us outside of ourselves into concern for others. To be wise is to be willing to reach beyond our own selfish self-seeking and to seek the best for others.

Wisdom teaches that the virtuous and wise life is characterized by generosity towards God and other people (Prov 3:9–10). It is impossible to be wise or virtuous without a concern for other people and especially for the poor (21:13, 15; 22:8). The wise person is not self-involved, but involved with others and seeks to benefit not just himself or herself, but others as well. This emphasis on concern for others is manifested in many ways. In the wisdom tradition acts of love overcome the impact of sin in our lives (16:6). Concern for the poor and powerless is a part of living wisely (31:9). Jesus summarizes this aspect of godly character in the Sermon on the Mount when he speaks of loving enemies:

> You have heard that it was said, "Love your neighbor and hate your enemy." But I tell you: Love your enemies and pray for those who persecute you, that you may be sons of your Father in heaven. He causes his sun to rise on the evil and the good, and sends rain on the righteous and the unrighteous. If you love those who love you, what reward

will you get? Are not even the tax collectors doing that? And if you greet only your brothers, what are you doing more than others? Do not even pagans do that? Be perfect, therefore, as your heavenly Father is perfect. (Matt 5:43–48)

Moral perfection is found in loving those whom we do not naturally love and showing concern for them. In order to fully embody wisdom, we must embody the kind of self-giving love that God displays towards us.

The Fullness and Variety of Virtue

No short chapter in a book like this can do justice to the variety of the virtues wisdom literature extolls. As mentioned earlier, it is a characteristic of the Modern Age to attempt to fully comprehend a subject by reducing the many to a single principle or set of principles. This is not possible in the case of biblical wisdom literature. The virtues of the Christian life are as mysterious and varied as the character of God. While we can attempt to set out a theory of virtues, we cannot fully reduce wisdom or virtue to a set of principles. The wise and good life can only be learned through a life-long relationship with God and others, characterized by the quest for wisdom and goodness. Certainly for Christians the three theological virtues of faith, hope, and love are supreme. Yet, the infinite challenges of life involve many virtues and can only be learned and achieved by a constant meditation on the infinite variety of teachings in Scripture. It is wisdom that gives us that capacity.

Questions for Reflection

1. If you were to make the decision to develop humility and a humble character, what do you think you would change? Who would you model yourself after, if anyone?

2. Have you ever made a decision while under the influence of alcohol, drugs, lust, or some other mood-altering substance or emotion? What was the result?

3. How careful are you in what you say to others? Can you think of a situation where you were not prudent, and your words turned out to be harmful to you, your family, or others?

4. In your mind, how important is concern for others in life? In what ways are you concerned for others and in what ways are you sometimes not concerned for others?

I walked by the field of a lazy person, the vineyard of one with no common sense. I saw that it was overgrown with nettles. It was covered with weeds, and its walls were broken down. Then, as I looked and thought about it, I learned this lesson: A little extra sleep, a little more slumber, a little folding of the hands to rest—then poverty will pounce on you like a bandit; scarcity will attack you like an armed robber.

Proverbs 24:30–34 (NLT)

10

The Life of Labor

There is nothing so characteristic of contemporary life as the intense importance men and woman place on work. Work has become more than a way to make a living and provide for a family. Many people find their identity in their work. A few find not only their identity in work but the meaning and purpose for their lives. For some people, work has become an idol, a part of created existence through which we try to give our lives meaning and purpose. Every so often someone points out that modern people spend more time at work than with their children or spouse. Based on time alone, our work is an area in which we human beings most need wisdom and have many opportunities to demonstrate wisdom or the lack thereof. What can we learn from wisdom literature concerning how we ought to behave in our complex socio-economic circumstances?

Paradoxically, there has probably been no time in human history in which more people worship leisure time and desire to avoid work or work hard enough to be able to "retire early" than our contemporary society. On the other hand, never before, especially in the West have more people worked on days that formerly were reserved for rest. As the Judeo-Christian consensus has weakened, businesses are open seven days a week and many people, especially managers, do the same. Clearly, we have lost touch with something important about the role of work and of rest and leisure in the wise life.

The Household as a Place of Work

Just as family life in the ancient world differed from ours, economic life was very different as well. The culture of ancient Israel was both agrarian and family-based. Just as the family was the fundamental social unit of society, the family was also the fundamental economic unit of society. The Bible gives many clues concerning the nature of economic life in ancient Israel. The creation narrative reveals that Cain was a farmer and Abel a shepherd. Later we learn that Abraham and the other patriarchs were shepherds, tending large flocks of sheep that were the foundation of their wealth. In Egypt, Joseph was familiar with a farming economy in which land was the fundamental source of wealth. The relatives of David were shepherds and, perhaps, small farmers. Throughout the Old Testament, the basic kind of economy with which the writers were familiar was an agricultural economy.

Where there is an agricultural economy, other occupations also emerge. In Israel, most farmers tended small plots of land and flocks. Some families accumulated enough land and herds to make their primary duty managerial. They employed farmers and shepherds who worked the land for them. Inevitably, farming communities developed other occupations: tradesmen, such as carpenters, small moneylenders, dealers in crops and foodstuffs, and traders who made their living trading clothing and household items for crops or domestic animals. In every small village there were merchants and small craftsmen. We know that Jesus' father, Joseph, was a carpenter and that the profession of carpentry existed in ancient Israel.[1] Together with carpentry, there were other craftsmen who made their living in this fundamentally agrarian economy.

In this kind of economy, everyone worked. Generally, men did the farming, or at least that part of the farming that took them away from the children and the environment of the household. Women and children helped with the farming, tended gardens, drew the

---

1. Gowan, *Bridge Between the Testaments*, 244–45.

water, provided for the meals, and made many of the necessities of life, like clothing. Even small children worked very hard by our standards.

Although women normally remained close to the home, most women, and especially women of poorer households, the so-called "people of the land," probably worked the fields with their husband and family, particularly during demanding times of planting and harvest. Women normally had little economic freedom, but they had some and one can imagine that many women made the most of that freedom. Proverbs 31 speaks of a woman who works from day to night and who "considers a field and buys it; with the fruits of her hands she plants a vineyard" (v. 16). This description of the perfect wife gives additional clues to the working of a successful household. This woman spins wool and flax and makes clothing, some of which she undoubtedly sells in the community. She provides food for the family, some of which comes from far away (v. 14). Because of her constant work, she is able to save a bit of money, and she invests that money wisely (v. 16). She understands that the merchandise she makes, presumably clothing, is in demand and works day and night at her spindle to earn more money for the household (vv. 18–19). She makes linen garments and sashes and sells them to nearby merchants (v. 24).

Ancient Israel was located in the Fertile Crescent, along the trade routes that connected Babylonia and Persia in the east, with Egypt in the south and west of Israel. As such, its cities and towns participated in the economic life of a trading culture that, even in the ancient world, extended beyond political boundaries. Eventually, what we would call "trading families" developed—families whose primary business was buying and selling merchandise.

The many references in Scripture to moneylending inform us that the business of moneylending existed in this primitive economy.[2] One can imagine that initially small merchants and farmers

---

2. Ancient rabbis permitted charging of interest to non-Jews. As to Jewish borrowers, interest *per se* was prohibited, though probably charged in certain

began extending credit and charging for its extension. Some of these businessmen and women became successful enough that money-lending became their primary occupation. In larger cities, where the economy was more complex, there were certainly banking families of considerable wealth.

While the world of the writers of wisdom literature was different than our world in many ways, it was also surprisingly similar. I can well remember long ago reading a contract drawn up when the Jews were in exile in Babylon hundreds of years before Christ was born and thinking to myself that this bill of sale was very similar to one I was working on in my office. While the professions were less sophisticated than in our day, the foregoing discussion shows that banking and finance and international trade were present in an embryonic form.

Jim and Jan are in their early thirties. Jim grew up in a professional family but partied his way through college. He has worked only intermittently since graduation. Jan grew up in a working class home. Her parents sacrificed to send her to a private college, where she worked hard and met her future husband. Since graduating, Jan has taught school and acquired a graduate degree at night which has helped her earn more in her job. The family is dependent upon Jan for both income and benefits such as health insurance. Jan would like to stop working for a few years to stay home with her two children, but that is impossible. Neither Jan nor Jim is a good financial manager. They have a significant amount of debt. Jim, accustomed to having parents with a high income, cannot understand why they must scrimp and barely get by. Jan, on the other hand, is increasingly upset by Jim's failure to work and watch his spending.

---

situations. Instead, a practice of partnership developed that permitted borrowing. (Berlin and Grossman, "Money Lending," 509.) Jesus tells parables concerning moneylenders, indicating their existence in the first century.

The Importance of Hard Work

There is nowhere that wisdom literature is more realistic than in the area of work. If there is to be economic security, there must also be productive hard work. Without work it is impossible to achieve economic security. One of the first ways in which the voice of wisdom in Proverbs is heard is in the form of the voice of a father warning his son against the dangers of laziness. The voice of the father exhorts the child (and by implication all children) to consider the work ethic of a colony of ants and emulate them:

> Go to the ant, O sluggard; consider her ways, and be wise. Without having any chief, officer, or ruler, she prepares her bread in summer and gathers her food in harvest. How long will you lie there, O sluggard? When will you arise from your sleep? A little sleep, a little slumber, a little folding of the hands to rest, and poverty will come upon you like a robber, and want like an armed man. (6:6–11 ESV)

The substance of this proverb is repeated over and over again, sometimes in humorous ways designed to teach the virtue of hard work (Prov 10:5; 12:24; 15:19; 19:24; 20:4, 13; 21:25–26).[3] A sluggard, one who fails to work hard, is portrayed as making excuses as ridiculous as using the imagined existence of a lion in the streets as a pretext for not getting up in the morning (22:13). He or she is portrayed as turning over and over in bed like a door swinging on its hinges (26:14).

The wise men and women of Israel constantly taught that a person who lies around expecting life to provide them an income is unwise. In fact, to the devout Jew one who failed to work hard was worse than foolish, such a person was morally lacking in some important way. This traditional view is echoed by Paul:

> In the name of the Lord Jesus Christ, we command you, brothers and sisters, to keep away from every believer who is idle and disruptive and does not live according to the teaching you received from us. For you yourselves know

3. Westermann, *Roots of Wisdom*, 20.

how you ought to follow our example. We were not idle when we were with you, nor did we eat anyone's food without paying for it. On the contrary, we worked night and day, laboring and toiling so that we would not be a burden to any of you. We did this, not because we do not have the right to such help, but in order to offer ourselves as a model for you to imitate. For even when we were with you, we gave you this rule: "The one who is unwilling to work shall not eat." (2 Thess 3:6–10)

Paul, the "Pharisee of Pharisees," was brought up with the work ethic of the ancient Jews who considered hard work central to the good life; any person who was unwilling to work long and hard was a fool.

Anyone who has worked on a farm or engaged in any form of manual labor knows that physical labor is difficult and not infrequently repetitive and boring. There is a constant temptation to rest, to stop, to find an easy way out, or to delay. In a primitive agrarian culture, laziness and poverty had a close relationship, as it does today—though the form and consequences of that poverty may differ. In a culture without a social security safety net, the consequences of failing to work hard and save was poverty in the short term and extreme poverty in old age. In a small town, where everyone knows everyone else's business, there would also be gossip about the person and social isolation (see Prov 14:20; 19:4b; 19:7).

There is another aspect of laziness and failure to work hard that emerges from wisdom literature. The lazy person is not only *disrespected* but also *dependent* on others and, therefore, not a free and independent person. The person who will not work must beg or borrow. Unfortunately, "The rich rule over the poor, and the borrower is the servant of the lender" (22:7). As a practical matter, right or wrong, those who are without debt possess more economic independence and liberty than those who are indebted, and therefore, economically dependent. This is an example of the intense realism of wisdom literature.

When it comes to work, wisdom literature is not primarily attempting to tell us how the world should be. Instead, the writers reflect on common human experience. Wisdom writers describe what the world is in fact like, and the underlying personal qualities necessary to successfully navigate human life. Hard work is necessary if wealth is to be created. Without hard work, there can be no security and only limited freedom. This is just the way the world is, and the experience of generations upon generations of people proves it to be so.

The Moral Quality of Wealth

The ancients did not perceive a strict division between practical and moral wisdom common among modern people. For wisdom writers, the acquisition and maintenance of wealth and the way in which wealth is used are matters fraught with intertwined economic and moral significance. They saw a reality we often miss: human beings live one life in one unified world. Its moral and practical aspects cannot be practically divided in life or in a person's consciousness without damage to both. In fact, since each moment of life is a single unity in which moral and practical aspects are joined in a single life, it cannot be divided at all in day-to-day living. We may for a time divide them for purposes of analysis, but our conclusions are put to work in one unified life.

Each person is one unified human soul. We cannot be a moral person one moment and an economic person unconcerned with the moral consequences of our behavior the next without damage to the person we are and are becoming. This insight is fundamental to recovering an understanding of the moral quality of our economic life. The philosopher Alfred North Whitehead, in his book *Adventures of Ideas* says, "A great society is a society in which men of business think greatly of their functions."[4] This is true: no society can be truly great in which its people do not think greatly of their day-to-day task

4. A. N. Whitehead, *Adventure of Ideas*, 98.

of working and earning a living. As we are learning, no society can be healthy unless people view their work and labor as a way of putting their faith and values to work for the good of all.

We human beings were meant to work, having been created to be the caretakers and stewards of God's good creation (Gen 1:28; 2:15). Jesus, when he was among us, speaks in John of the importance of his work when he says, "I must work the works of him that sent me, while it is day for the night cometh, when no man can work" (John 9:4). Paul encourages believers to work, and records that even as an evangelist he practiced his old profession as a tent maker (1 Cor 9:14). Paul also encouraged his followers to work and work hard (2 Thess 3:10). The Bible is full of encouragement for believers to work hard at their chosen labor.

Righteousness and Economic Security

A noticeable feature of wisdom literature is the connection it draws between righteousness and economic security. The power of the rich is something that wisdom literature accepts while noting that there are moral limits to the power that the rich should have over the poor:

> The person who oppresses the poor insults the One who created him and gave him life; the person who is kind to the poor and shows them mercy honors the One who made him or her." (Prov 14:31; author's paraphrase)

The wealthy do have economic power, but the wise and righteous person does not abuse it.

Riches are a good thing, but riches can disappear unexpectedly. Therefore, the wise person does not rely upon wealth for meaning and purpose in life, let alone salvation in times of trouble (11:4). The wise person understands there are limits to what can and ought to be done in the search for wealth and economic security. In the end, our ultimate security in life cannot be found in our wealth. We will return to this theme of wisdom literature later.

Jesus reinforced this truth in his parable of the rich fool, warning his followers against the perils of greed (Luke 12:15). As Jesus told the story, there was a rich man who attempted to seek security in his wealth. He had an abundant crop, and so determined to build bigger barns in order to store the crop and be able to be at ease for many, many years (v. 19). God, however, had different plans, and told him that the hour of his death had come (v. 20). The story concludes, "This is how it will be with anyone who stores up things for himself but is not rich toward God" (v. 21). Wealth, as important as it may be, cannot give life meaning and purpose, nor can it secure us against the ultimate uncertainty created by our own mortality.

Honesty and Fair Dealing in Economic Affairs

As mentioned previously, honesty and fair dealing are important in conducting business affairs. In Proverbs we read, "False weights and unequal measures—the Lord detests double standards of every kind" (20:10 NLT). The ancient writers were familiar with dishonest dealings, and they condemned them. They are not only wrong and a bad business practice, but they also offend God and the moral order God embedded in the universe. No one trusts a dishonest person.

The story of the dealings between Laban and Jacob is instructive. Jacob served his uncle Laban for seven years, and then was tricked into consummating his marriage with the wrong woman. He served another seven years in order to receive the wife he desired. When he wanted to leave, his uncle persuaded him to stay. During this entire time, Laban changed Jacob's wages and took advantage of him (Gen 31:7). Finally, Jacob struck a bargain with Laban: Laban would continue to receive the white colored sheep, which were the most valuable. Jacob, however, would receive the speckled, spotted, or dark colored sheep. Jacob then bred Laban's cattle in such a way that Jacob was enriched while Laban became poorer.[5] In the end, while Jacob

---

5. The complicated story of the relationship between Jacob and Laban is recorded in Genesis 29:1—31:25.

was enriched by his scheme, the attitude of Laban and his family towards Jacob changed. Jacob has succeeded in his scheme, but he has forfeited the love and respect of his uncle.

This biblical story could easily be a parable for much contemporary economic life. While many, many people attempt to deal fairly with others, too many people view our economy as a vast arena of conflict in which the primary goal is to gain for one's self at the expense of others. Frequently, business is compared to warfare, as is evidenced by constant references to the Chinese classic *The Art of War* in much discussion about business. This analogy is both misleading and inaccurate. Our economic life is about providing for our families and ourselves. It is not essentially warfare at all. When it becomes warfare, as it often has become in the modern world, something is deeply amiss. What is essentially a way in which we provide for our families and live in community with others becomes something that destroys harmony and creates social, international, and personal friction.[6] When business becomes a kind of warfare of producers against consumers, employees against management, the wealthy against the poor and middle class, something important and basic has been lost.

Many years ago, I read the story of one of the founders of the oil industry who was renowned for his success as an oilman and business executive. In the article he bemoaned the changes he had seen in business during the course of his lifetime. One change he described was from a time when one did not need written contracts because people kept their promises even when they might suffer a loss, to the current situation where almost every transaction requires lawyers to prepare "ironclad" contracts, which, of course, many people proceed to break anyway.

---

6. The communitarian and relational aspects of biblical wisdom compared with the individualistic and power-oriented character of much modern business practice can be an important Christian contribution to economic theory, business theory, and business ethics.

The Virtue of Generosity

Interestingly, an important teaching in Proverbs related to economic matters concerns the first use of the proceeds of economic life. "Honor the Lord with your wealth, and with the first fruits of all your crops, then your barns will be filled to overflowing, and your vines will brim over with new wine" (3:9–10). Deep within the wisdom view of economic life is the connection between generosity (giving to God and to others) and economic blessing. There is a deep connection between personal generosity and economic wisdom. Proverbs teaches, "One person gives freely, and grows richer and more wealthy; another person withholds what he or she should give and grows poorer to the point of being in need" (11:24; author's paraphrase). The generous person is more connected to the fundamental economic principles God has embedded in the universe than a person who is greedy and withholds giving.

Why is generosity so important? One answer involves the power riches have to distort our thinking and perspective. As we become more affluent, there is a danger that we will begin to believe that our riches are the fundamental source of our personal security. The wisdom writers believe this belief involves a fundamentally foolish way of thinking. "Riches do not profit in the day of wrath, but righteousness delivers from death" (Prov 11:4). Ultimately, righteousness before God, and not money, is our source of security.

Anyone who has been in business for any length of time has met people who before they were successful were faithful church attenders, prayerful, and relatively generous. Unfortunately, when success came, they relied more and more upon their economic power to give them security and gradually lost the humble faithfulness that provided them the character that was at the foundation of their success. Years ago, I knew such a person. How tragic it was to see the gradual deterioration of the personality of this fundamentally fine person.

There is, however, a deeper foundation for showing generosity than its moral impact in overcoming our natural selfishness. In generosity, as in showing mercy to the poor and giving them justice, we live in accordance with the deep relationality of the universe God created. The rich and the poor are connected by a common humanity—a humanity that none of us can escape or diminish (Ps 42:9). Human beings cannot disturb this deep relationality without being themselves diminished in some way.

For most of my adult life, I have lived in large cities, where the middle class and wealthy are able to create enclaves that protect them against contact with poorer communities. The nature of our modern economic system means that the upper middle class can live for long periods without coming into any meaningful contact with the poor. In our early forties, we were privileged to live in a small town where it is less possible to separate one's self from the community, including the poor. This experience made me more aware of the way in which the rich and poor inevitably inhabit a common social space.

Today, we live in a city in which there is racial and social division, and in which many in the upper and middle classes move into separately incorporated communities. At the same time, our city has difficulty attracting quality employers. Many of those employers cite the workforce, a lack of workers available to hire for entry-level, production, or factory jobs, as a reason not to relocate in our community. Of course, this means that there are fewer jobs for managers and other skilled personnel. What is sometimes missing in public debates about jobs and economic development is an understanding that we are all related. One part of a metropolitan community cannot be healthy if the other parts are weak or sick.[7]

There may be no area in which a wisdom approach to social problems is more important than in the area of economic life. As I write, we Americans are in the midst of an enormous "deleveraging" caused by the kind of excessive debt that wisdom literature warns against. That economic crisis was caused both by citizens borrowing

7. Scruggs, "Lack of Good Jobs," M3–M4.

more than they could possibly repay—and by the greed of those who loaned them the money. Our economic system is not self-sufficient or self-sustaining. It rests on a moral foundation. Without people who work hard, take care of their families, save, and provide for others, and a government that does the same, no economic system can work properly.

Wisdom literature does not provide us with a detailed blueprint for modern economic life. Instead, it provides basic practical, moral, and spiritual principles to guide human beings in ordering their economic affairs. These principles leave open vast areas of freedom within which different groups of people and societies can structure their economic lives. We cannot successfully structure our lives in violation of these fundamental principles. There is no such thing as a stable home, family, business, or government that has excessive levels of debt or fails to value hard work, saving, generosity, and the like.

Questions for Reflection

1. Do you think of your work as a part of your family life, as part of providing for yourself, parents, and children, or as something else?

2. Can you think of a time when you departed from the "rule of fair dealing" only to find that you had harmed yourself and others?

3. In your view, does generosity—giving to the poor, to your church, and other charities—help or hurt your economic life? How much power does greed have over your life?

4. Do you accept the view that the poor and the rich are related to one another by their common humanity and are therefore connected in a deep way, such that justice for both is required by God?

When the righteous prosper, the city rejoices; when the wicked perish, there are shouts of joy. Through the blessing of the upright a city is exalted, but by the mouth of the wicked it is destroyed.

PROVERBS 11:10–11

By making just and righteous decisions, those in authority give stability to a community of people. When those in authority take bribes the community is ruined.

PROVERBS 29:4 (AUTHOR'S PARAPHRASE)

11

Life in Community

In his book *Profiles in Courage*, John Kennedy tells the story of Edmund Ross, a Republican senator from Kansas who cast the deciding vote ending impeachment proceedings against President Andrew Johnson.[1] When Lincoln was assassinated, Johnson followed Lincoln's moderate policy toward the South. Impeachment proceedings began when radical Republicans passed a Tenure of Office Act preventing the president from firing cabinet members without Senate consent. The specific case was Edwin Stanton, who opposed Johnson's policies.

Johnson felt the wise course was to readmit Southern States into the Union as quickly as possible. Stanton disagreed. When Johnson fired Stanton, impeachment proceedings began. The House voted impeachment and the trial moved to the Senate. Senator Ross took the position that, while he had no sympathy for Johnson, Johnson deserved a fair trial. Ultimately, Ross voted against conviction, reasoning that if a president could be forced out of office because of a policy disagreement, the power of the presidency would be eliminated. Ross's action unleashed relentless criticism. He was not re-elected and suffered greatly. His behavior was an example of political courage.

1. For the full story, see Kennedy, *Profiles in Courage*, 115–38.

The media constantly asks, "Where are the leaders?" Confidence in the political leadership and the structure of Western democracies has never been lower. People feel that their leaders lack both concern for the average person and basic moral qualities, such as honesty. Is there anything we can learn from the pre-modern writers of wisdom literature that could help our fragile community life? The answer is, "Yes."

Wisdom and Leadership in Israel

As mentioned earlier, one purpose of wisdom literature was to train those who would ultimately become a part of Israel's government. Therefore, it is not surprising that wisdom literature contains specific advice concerning government and leadership. On the other hand, given that a specific intention of wisdom literature is the training of future government officials, the limited amount and nature of the advice given is surprising. Only a limited number of wisdom passages specifically address issues of government. Most of the advice is general and moral in nature. Some issues that all governments face are not addressed at all. Why is this so?

In order to understand biblical wisdom and its application in contemporary society, it is important to consider the nature of government during the time of the Israelite kings. The patriarchs were tribal leaders. Abraham, for example, is portrayed as the leader of a tribe made up of related family members, their wives, children, and servants. His descendants, Isaac and Jacob, are likewise tribal leaders.

Genesis ends with the story of Joseph, one of the sons of Israel, who dreams of ruling over his brothers. He suffers near death, slavery, betrayal, and imprisonment, before his elevation as the senior advisor to Pharaoh of Egypt. His ability to interpret dreams and give practical advice to Pharaoh results in his advancement. The story of Joseph is the story of how wisdom and practical ability can bring a person into leadership in a time of crisis.

Exodus describes the deliverance of Israel from Egypt as a nation of thousands of people belonging to tribes associated with the twelve sons of Jacob. Moses was a charismatic leader who emerged from the tribe of Levi, not the most prominent tribe, as a person commissioned by God to lead the tribes of Israel. He tried unsuccessfully to personally handle all the business of the wandering tribes. This situation could not last very long. When his father-in-law arrived to see his family, the man was moved to give some very practical advice. When his father-in-law, Jethro, saw how Moses was trying to lead the people, he gave Moses advice that begins the emergence of a post-tribal governmental structure for Israel:

> What you are doing is not good. You and these people who come to you will only wear yourselves out. The work is too heavy for you; you cannot handle it alone. Listen now to me and I will give you some advice, and may God be with you. You must be the people's representative before God and bring their disputes to him. Teach them the decrees and laws, and show them the way to live and the duties they are to perform. But select capable men from all the people— men who fear God, trustworthy men who hate dishonest gain—and appoint them as officials over thousands, hundreds, fifties and tens. Have them serve as judges for the people at all times, but have them bring every difficult case to you; the simple cases they can decide themselves. That will make your load lighter, because they will share it with you. If you do this and God so commands, you will be able to stand the strain, and all these people will go home satisfied. (Exod 18:17b–23)

The system of government suggested by Jethro involved adding a formal leadership group to what was an essentially tribal system of government.

From the time of Moses through the conquest of the land under Joshua, this pattern of a charismatic leader chosen by God providing leadership by force of character in cooperation with tribal leaders worked. Once the people had conquered the land of Israel, and the tribes did not have to work together to survive, the system began to break down. The book of Judges describes this gradual breakdown. The book ends with this pessimistic description of Israel on the eve of Saul and David: "In those days, Israel had no king; everyone did as he saw fit" (Judg 21:25). The tribal, charismatic system broke down under the pressure of new political realities. It simply could not provide for domestic or foreign security.

By the end of the leadership of Samuel, the people wanted a king. First, Saul was chosen king. After he proved unworthy, David succeeded him. Although Saul and David are portrayed in Scripture as very different sorts of people, in some ways Saul and David are similar figures. Samuel, the final charismatic judge over Israel, raised both of them to the kingship through anointment. Their legitimacy was partially dependent upon their charismatic anointing by Samuel and by their personal reflection of that charisma.

Despite their charismatic anointing, Saul and David relied upon support of the tribal elders of Israel, and the loss by Solomon's son of the support of the ten northern tribes seems to have caused the end of the unified kingdom (1 Kgs 12:1–16).[2] Neither Saul nor David, nor any other king of Israel, fully supplanted the tribal system. Solomon was the most successful in this respect, but his death was followed by tribal revolt.

This brief overview makes it plain that ancient Israel was a far cry from a modern nation-state. It was a loose confederation of tribes connected to one another by their acknowledged common descent from the patriarchs. A king ruled because the tribes that composed Israel needed to defend themselves against surrounding tribes, then increasingly against kingdoms such as Assyria, Egypt, Babylonia, and the like. In order to retain power, the king was, however, dependent on cooperation and support from tribal leaders. The bureaucratic

2. The essentially tribal nature of David's kingdom is underscored by the words of the ten northern tribes upon their revolt against Reheboam's foolish harshness: "What part do we have in David, what part in Jesse's son? To your tents, O Israel! Look after your own house, O David!" (1 Kgs 12:16).

requirements of such a kingdom were a far cry from those required for a modern nation-state. The complexity of the modern nation-state can obscure an important foundational insight modern political science too easily misses: to be successful, government must be both moral and wise.

Wisdom and Government

Wisdom literature begins its teachings on government exactly where one thinks it might: by establishing the vital importance of wisdom in establishing and maintaining good government. In Proverbs 8 we read, "By me kings reign and rulers issue decrees that are just; by me princes govern, and nobles—all who rule on earth" (vv. 15–16). A stable government is founded on the same principle as a stable life. Leaders must have shrewd insight into the world, an understanding of the moral foundations of society, and the capacity to translate that insight into action.

When I was young, a movie was made in which a teenager became president of the United States.[3] *Wild in the Streets* reflected the revolutionary and unrealistic culture of its day, positing what might happen if young people were able to hold higher office. Perhaps unintentionally it made an important point concerning the dangers associated with immature and inexperienced leadership. The wisdom writers understood that leaders are faced with matters of existential importance, issues of war and peace, of the level of taxation a people can bear, of the proper regulation of economic and other affairs. In order to judge these matters wisely, a person must have some level of understanding, wisdom, and experience in life and in government. Otherwise, the people of the nation will be ill-protected and impoverished.

3. *Wild in the Streets*, American International Pictures, 1968.

The Essential Moral Quality of Government

Almost all discussion of government in wisdom literature is ethical in nature. For the writers of wisdom literature, the fundamental duty of government was to secure justice and undergird the moral foundations of society. "When the righteous prosper, the city rejoices; when the wicked perish, there are shouts of joy. Through the blessing of the upright a city is exalted, but by the mouth of the wicked it is destroyed" (Prov 11:10–11; see also 28:21; 31:4). Because wisdom literature sees morality as a real and important quality, it perceives the maintenance and support of morality as an essential governmental task.

In the administration of justice, judges and other public officials bear special responsibility to resist wickedness and avoid persecution of the righteous. Proverbs teaches: "One who justifies the wicked and one who condemns the righteous are both alike an abomination to the Lord" (17:15 NRSV). A governmental official who favors the rich or the poor, who fails to judge fairly, or who decides on the basis of friendship or a bribe, "justifies the wicked" or "condemns the righteous." Such a person acts contrary to the moral order God established and is abominable to the One who is just and fair in all dealings (Prov 17:26). In this respect, social justice and care for the poor are essential elements of the wisdom tradition.

From a wisdom perspective, the rise and fall of nations is essentially connected to the fundamental moral and ethical responsibilities of government. "Righteousness exalts a nation, but sin is a reproach to any people" (11:34 RSV). When wise and ethical leadership guide a nation, it prospers; when such leaders fail to guide it, it faces judgment and decline.[4] The sin that undermines a government is both social and individual. In order for a society to be stable, the individuals within the society must be just; and the moral basis of

4. The history of Israel recorded in 1 and 2 Kings and 1 and 2 Chronicles is founded on the insight that a failure by a government or people to be guided by ideals of wisdom and morality results in the decline of a people and ultimate suffering for citizens.

the society as a whole must reflect and support righteousness among its members.

In this respect, wisdom literature is both individualistic and communitarian in its outlook. There can be no virtuous society without virtuous people, and virtuous people cannot live happily and prosperously in a society lacking virtue. Wisdom literature avoids both extreme individualism and extreme communitarianism. People need a just society—and a just society needs ethical citizens. A stable society is founded on the virtue of individuals, nuclear and extended families, social organizations, and society as a whole. Each aspect of society is both independent and interdependent. Underlying wisdom literature is a deeply relational view of government and society—in which social stability and individual responsibility are not separate but related phenomena. There can be no sharp distinction between private morality and public action. They are each dependent upon the existence of the other. This is an insight that we desperately need to understand in contemporary society.

The Role of Wise Advice in Government

As one might expect from a curriculum designed to train government officials, wisdom literature places a premium on a ruler getting the kind of wise advice he or she needs. "Plans fail for lack of counsel, but with many advisers they succeed" (Prov 15:22) and "Where there is no guidance, a people falls, but in an abundance of counselors there is safety" (11:14 RSV). A wise king values wise, righteous, and good advice (Prov 14:34–35; 16:11). No one can see all implications of a course of action, so a wise ruler gets good advice and plenty of it! This is especially true in matters of war and peace (20:18).

The quality of a ruler is largely determined by the quality of the advice the ruler receives. If a king receives foolish advice, or self-seeking advice, it affects the ability of the ruler to make wise decisions. Flattery and false speaking is a danger to a ruler and to his or her people (17:7, 15; 29:12). A ruler who only listens to advice that confirms his or her prejudices is not a wise ruler and will eventually fail.

This particular aspect of wisdom teaching is illustrated by the events that transpired on the death of Solomon. When Solomon died, there was a generational change in leadership. During his long reign, Solomon increasingly taxed his people to pay for his public projects. The ten northern tribes, who were not bound to the house of David by historic, tribal ties wanted Solomon's son, Rehoboam to lighten the burden of taxation and forced labor that Solomon had placed on them (1 Kgs 12:4). Solomon's more experienced advisors suggested that Rehoboam comply with this request (vv. 6–7). The younger advisors not only recommended that Rehoboam refuse, but also suggested an offensive answer (vv. 10–11). Rehoboam listened to the advice of his younger, less experienced advisors (vv. 12–15). The result was the division of the Ten Northern Tribes from the tribes of Judah and Benjamin (vv. 16–21).

How nice it would be if anyone could effectively run a government and lead a society. Unfortunately, this is not true. A leader, however well intentioned, must be personally qualified for his or her position and surrounded by persons who give wise advice. There is no single person who can possibly have all the knowledge needed to run even the smallest unit of society, much less its larger governmental organs. If the person chosen to lead has sufficient experience—the more the better—this is most helpful. Those who can make up for the limitations of the leader must surround a person who leads.

The Importance of the Judicial System

One of the most serious failings of any government is its inability or unwillingness to provide justice to citizens. The teachings of the Mosaic Law were clear that it is wrong to deprive anyone, rich or poor of justice (Exod 23:2–6; Lev 19:15; Deut 1:17). Judges are to be impartial. The poor are not to be denied justice because of their poverty nor are the rich to be denied justice because of their wealth. In the final chapter of Proverbs we are told to "Speak up for those who cannot speak for themselves; ensure justice for those being crushed. Yes, speak up for the poor and helpless, and see that they get justice" (31:8–9). This could be extended by implication to any distinction among persons—economic, racial, religious, and otherwise—unrelated to the issue at hand. Partiality in deciding pubic matters is contrary to the moral law and to the interests of a prosperous and stable government (see 24:23).

One common form of partiality is the tendency of those in power to favor those who can do them the most good—the rich. This is to be avoided. A wise judge never "closes his ears to the cries of the poor" (21:13) and "If a king judges the poor with fairness, his throne will be established forever" (29:14). In focusing on impartiality in the administration of justice, wisdom literature continues a preoccupation of the Torah (Exod 23:2–3, 9).

Another way by which a judicial system can be perverted is through bribery and perjury. Wisdom literature teaches that "By justice a king gives stability to the land; but one who exacts gifts ruins it" (Prov 29:4 RSV) and "A corrupt witness mocks at justice" (Prov 19:28). Over and over again, the dangers of bribery and false witness are highlighted by wisdom literature (12:17; 14:5, 25; 17:8, 23; 19:5; 21:28).

The goal of a judicial system is justice; and in order to secure justice, it must be led by a concern for truthfulness, with fairness, and with a concern to avoid prejudice and favoritism of any kind. Proverbs teaches:

> Partiality in judging is not good. Whoever says to the wicked, "You are in the right," will be cursed by peoples, abhorred by nations, but those who rebuke the wicked will have delight, and a good blessing will come upon them. Whoever gives an honest answer kisses the lips. (24:23–26 ESV)

Wise government requires an impartial, wise, righteous, and honest judicial system. Judges and other public officials must seek the truth in circumstances and justice in action, so that the reality of a concrete situation is reflected in their decision, not personal preference or corruption.

Wisdom in a World of Conflict

One striking aspect of Jewish wisdom literature is the lack of specific advice about armed conflict. The narrative portions of the Old Testament reflect war and conflict, and certainly the character of David reflects that of a warrior prince. However, the kind of advice about war present in Chinese wisdom literature, such as the *Tao Te Ching* or *The Art of War*, is absent in biblical wisdom literature.[5] Wise kings are careful to consider wise advice when waging war, and they must listen to wise counsel in its conduct (Prov 20:18; 24:5–6). Detailed advice about war or its conduct is absent in biblical wisdom literature. This is probably due to the simple fact that, for most of its history, Israel was not a large or powerful nation. It was, in fact, surrounded by warlike nations like the Philistines, the Assyrians, the Babylonians, and the like. Under such circumstances, the best course of action was to avoid conflict.

The ancient Middle East was, like the Middle East today, a region of frequent conflict. The kingdom of David did participate in the wars of the region. Nevertheless, biblical faith never fully accommodated itself to this reality. Even in the Old Testament, the biblical writers preferred peace to war, reflecting the character of the God of peace (Ps 120:7). War, if it has a purpose, serves to restore a preexisting state of peace.

The Old Testament suspicion of war and aggression, finds a kind of completion in the New Testament. Jesus teaches that it is the peacemakers who will be blessed (Matt 5:9). James teaches that the cause of conflict, domestic and foreign, is the desire for that which

---

5. Neither the *Tao Te Ching* nor the *Art of War*, of course, plays the same religious role in Chinese culture that the Bible plays among Christians. Both are, however, honored texts of their culture.

belongs to another (Jas 4:1–4). Thus, a suspicion of war in the Old Testament is deepened by New Testament wisdom.

The Way of Wisdom in the Postmodern World

Wisdom literature certainly does not provide a simple roadmap for contemporary political activity. The agrarian culture of the Old Testament is far removed from contemporary Western democracy. Modern leaders oversee a nation made up of city dwellers who are part of a complex industrial and post-industrial economy. However, wisdom principles are as essential a foundation for contemporary governments as for the government of ancient Israel.

Moral decay and injustice still erode the foundations of society. Moral values continue to be important for leaders. Leaders still need good character and a willingness to listen to good advice. Wise leaders are still concerned about the integrity of the political system and especially of the courts. Just as in the days of ancient Israel, it is easy for a government to pay attention to the needs of the wealthy and well-connected—and hard, sometimes incredibly hard, to listen to the cries of the poor.

Michael Polanyi, whose works have been referred to previously, points out a paradox: modern society often combines a cynical disregard for truth and moral values with fanatical devotion to certain moral ideals or an ideology, right or left. The Russian Communists and German Nazis were equally inspired by an ideological moral fervor cut off from a deep, rich philosophical, religious, and moral basis in a history and tradition that could guide it and allow it to be self-critical. The search for a just society, cut off from a deep belief in justice and other values, allows practitioners of modern ideological politics to embrace a fanaticism that permits acts of gross immorality in the search for a better or perfect society.[6] The result is a loss of the moral and relational bonds that hold a complex society together.

6. Polanyi's *Science, Faith and Society* contains an extended argument as to the realities and dangers of this aspect of modern thinking.

Western democracies, with the roots of their cultural history in the Judeo-Christian tradition, need to recover a connection with the moral tradition of the West before the Enlightenment as it relates to the conduct of political affairs. Most importantly, Western culture would profit from recovering faith in justice as an aspect of reality that is progressively uncovered in the search for it in the concrete day-to-day business of government. In his book *Logic of Liberty*, Polanyi puts the matter in this way:

> The general foundations of coherence and freedom in society may be regarded as secure to the extent to which men uphold their belief in the reality of truth, justice, charity, and tolerance, and accept dedication to the service of these realities; while society may be expected to fall into servitude when men deny, explain away or simply disregard these realities and transcendent obligations.
>
> . . .
>
> We may be faced with the fact that only by resuming the great tradition which embodies faith in these realities can the continuance of the human race on earth, equipped with the powers of modern science be made both possible and desirable.[7]

If there is no such thing as truth and justice, if we are not constrained in our political behavior by a transcendent obligation to seek truth and justice in our political lives with tolerance for other views, then the state can and must dictate these matters. A society that has lost its belief in transcendent ideals has turned onto a road leading to tyranny. If, however, a society believes in the reality of transcendent moral and ethical ideals such as truth, justice, tolerance, and charity, and serves these ideals, the foundation of a free society can be maintained even in the face of conflict and uncertainty.[8]

7. Polanyi, *Logic of Liberty*, 57.
8. The term "reality" is used here as referring to intellectual and moral ideals that act as a goal and as an active component of decision-making. These intellectual and moral ideals, such as "truth" and "justice" exist independently of our subjective choice and are progressively revealed as we participate in the

Much of the frenetic dishonesty of contemporary politics comes from an underlying assumption of the right and left that there is nothing more fundamental involved than the contention of special interest groups for advantage. In the absence of faith in the reality of moral constraints on the political process and upon what special interest groups may legitimately seek, as well as upon what means may be used to seek them, a free and just society cannot endure.

If citizens and leaders believe in something called the "public interest" as an invisible reality which can and will be disclosed to us as we seek the invisible but progressively attainable reality of a more just order for society, then a free society can be maintained in the face of the trials and tests of human history. In such a society the voice of religious leaders can and should be heard in the public arena, for "Where there is no prophetic vision the people cast off restraint, but blessed is he who keeps the law" (Prov 29:18 ESV).

Modern advocates of a purely secular state may immediately suspect that any attempt to subject government to religious opinions and moral rules involves an attempt to set up a theocracy or "moralocracy." In fact, any attempt by religious or moral leaders to acquire political power as such would be contrary to the tradition of wisdom and politics. A society in which moral values guide leaders is a society in which leaders have been trained in wisdom and in the principles of moral leadership and instinctively bring them to bear upon the problems of the day. The role of morality and religion is primarily to create a kind of character in leaders, not to mandate a particular moral position in law. The condition of our society and its progressive social decline give evidence of consequences of the loss of wisdom tradition in Western democratic politics. Whether it can be recovered remains to be seen.

A wise society respects the many social units of which it is comprised. Families, neighborhoods, communities, churches, social organizations, and smaller governmental units each have a part to play

disciplined attempt to uncover them as part of a community of inquiry and practice.

in achieving a just and humane society. One of the chief functions of what might seem to be higher levels of organization is to nurture and respect the independence and functioning of private and local institutions. This is a challenge for the modern, secular state that is constantly faced with the temptation to usurp the power, position, and prerogative of what are called "mediating institutions" and private areas of social organization.

Questions for Reflection

1. In political science classes professors sometimes distinguish between "real politics," which means politics practiced without moral guidance solely on the basis of practicality. Do the writers of wisdom literature agree with this distinction?

2. The Bible teaches that for a government to be successful it must have a moral underpinning. Do you agree? What can provide such a moral underpinning?

3. One of the most frequent teachings of the wisdom writers concerns the importance of wise counsel for leaders. Why is wise counsel so important for leaders?

4. What happens to a nation when the judicial system is perverted?

The words of the Teacher, son of David, king in Jerusalem: "Meaning-less! Meaningless!" says the Teacher. "Utterly meaningless! Everything is meaningless."

ECCLESIASTES 1:1–2

He has made everything beautiful in its time. He has also set eternity in the human heart; yet no one can fathom what God has done from beginning to end.

ECCLESIASTES 3:11

Now all has been heard; here is the conclusion of the matter: Fear God and keep his commandments, for this is the duty of all mankind.

ECCLESIASTES 12:13

12

Does Wisdom Matter?

Many people consider Winston Churchill to be the greatest person of the twentieth century. Many people know that he was the Prime Minister of Great Britain during the Second World War. Others know of his oratorical skills. Fewer know that he was a great writer, and the author of highly regarded histories, including histories of the English speaking peoples and of World War II. Fewer still know that he was an above average painter. His life and career began near the end of the Victorian era and extended until the 1960s. He served in many important positions. He played a leadership role in Great Britain during most of the last century until his death. He retired from Parliament at ninety years of age. Near the end of his life, as he pondered his life and the decline of Britain, he exclaimed over and over again, "All has been for nothing."[1]

If this great man could not find ultimate meaning and purpose in his life and achievements, which were so many and varied, how can any of us expect to create meaning and purpose for our lives? The question explored by Ecclesiastes concerns the limitations upon our human capacity to create meaning for our lives. Ecclesiastes begins with the memorable line, "Meaningless, meaningless, says the Teacher. Utterly meaningless! Everything is meaningless" (Eccl 1:1; 12:8). The writer of Ecclesiastes explores the reality that wisdom and

1. Toye, *Churchill's Empire*, 303.

its accomplishments do not guarantee happiness, meaning, or purpose in life.

The Problems Addressed by Ecclesiastes

Ecclesiastes is often misunderstood. Contrary to some interpretations, the book is not a rejection of wisdom or of the life of righteousness. Instead it grapples with the limits of human wisdom and human striving. Specifically, Ecclesiastes deals with important issues that concerned ancient wisdom teachers and still concern us today:

1. Does life have any real meaning?

2. How can the unhappiness and failure of many successful people be squared with a teaching that holds that wisdom and righteousness will be rewarded and folly and evil punished?

The writer speaks of exhaustion in the search for wisdom and of the impossibility of finding a final answer to the important questions life poses. However, the Teacher still upholds the importance of the search for wisdom. "Wisdom, like an inheritance, is a good thing, and benefits those who see the sun" (7:11). The ultimate message of Ecclesiastes is not a denial of the value of the wise life. It is a discussion of the limits of wisdom.

Practical wisdom has its limits. It can only profit us in the practical things of life. Practical wisdom cannot answer life's most difficult questions. Human wisdom alone cannot answer questions involving the meaning and purpose of life, the reason for suffering, and the often-dubious moral nature of the universe. The search for wisdom is a human enterprise, and like all human enterprises, it is limited by our human finitude, sin, and shortcomings.

Allen is sitting alone in his office late at night. He recently learned that he has cancer and will live but a few more months. Over the past thirty years, Allen has built a fairly large company and is, by any standard, a wealthy person.

He has several homes, a private airplane, and many of the outward signs of wealth. For a time when he was younger, he kept a mistress. His success was not without cost. He worked long hours and sacrificed time with his family and children. By the time his children were in college, they were all more or less estranged from him. His son, who he once hoped would take over the family business, has not been home for several years and lives in a different state. Some years ago, his wife left him—tired of living alone with a man who most often ignored her. Since the divorce, Allen has spent most of his time working. Not so long ago, he was visiting with his lawyer about his will. It was a very difficult conversation. Finally, the lawyer looked at him and said, "Allen, you are trying to run your business from the grave—and you cannot do that. No one can. When you die, it is all over." Over the past few days, Allen has come to see the wisdom of that remark, and his years of work seem wasted. "I have just a few months to live, and I have to wind down this business or sell it to someone else. My life's work is wasted."

The Author of Wisdom as Critic

Ecclesiastes begins with the inscription: "The words of the Teacher, son of David, king in Jerusalem" (1:1a). Just as Proverbs is attached to the name of Solomon, reputedly the wisest person who ever lived, so also Ecclesiastes is attributed to King Solomon.[2] This attribution, whether or not it reflects the actual authorship of the book, clearly reflects its implied author to be Solomon. By this inscription, a reader is invited to regard the author as a king, and a special kind of king: a king who is experienced in the questions and quandaries of life and also a teacher of God's people. As one who supremely embodies the

2. Many scholars place the date of Ecclesiastes as late as the third century BC. Others place the book earlier. When exactly it was written does not really matter. What matters is that the book is attributed to Solomon as the patron of wisdom literature in the Old Testament and in Israel.

program of the wisdom school of Israel, the author reflects upon its limitations.

Does Human Life Make Sense?

Ecclesiastes begins with an observation: "Generations come and generations go, but the earth never changes" (1:4 NLT). We human beings are born, we labor to provide for our families, we try to make a difference, we seek to find ultimate meaning in our accomplishments, but the world resists all of our efforts to create meaning and purpose. All our attempts to find meaning and purpose for our lives in the end appear to come to nothing.

The Teacher begins his quest for meaning by seeking wisdom. Wisdom, in the end, is about understanding life. The Teacher diligently studies, observes, and reflects upon life. But, the complexities of life are too great. "What is twisted cannot be straightened; what is lacking cannot be counted" (Eccl 1:15). Life defies our attempts to understand it from beginning to end. In the end, the Teacher has to admit that achieving complete wisdom is beyond human capacity (7:23).

Faced with the realization that the search for wisdom is unending and ultimately fruitless, the Teacher seeks, like many modern people, to find meaning in pleasure. He eats and drinks to his heart's content (2:1–2). He exercises his human abilities, building houses and gardens, acquiring flocks and herds, and planting crops and fruit trees (vv. 4–7). He amasses great wealth (v. 8). He acquires slaves and has many women (vv. 7–8). The Teacher denies himself nothing his heart desires, but in the end, it is all meaningless (vv. 10–11). Finally, faced with the despair inherent in a life of pleasure seeking, like a postmodern Westerner, he even embraces madness—but this too is folly (vv. 12–16).

In the end, like a burned-out shell, the Teacher gives up. The search for meaning and purpose, whether by wisdom or foolishness, by work or leisure, by the search for beauty or a life of self-denial, fails. In the end, the Teacher concludes that the most reasonable thing a human being can do is enjoy the simple pleasures of life and accept what comes from the hand of God (vv. 24–26).

The kind of life that the Teacher leads prior to this realization is the kind of life that philosopher Soren Kierkegaard describes as the "aesthetic life"—a life driven by a search for pleasure and personal self-fulfillment.[3] People who embrace a search for meaning and purpose in life by seeking personal accomplishments, personal pleasure (whether physical, mental, or emotional) end up, if they are wise, facing the fact that such a life is ultimately meaningless. The search for meaning through pleasure and human accomplishment is doomed to failure.

Wisdom, for all of its value, cannot by itself answer the biggest questions of life. As much as we wish that simply "being good and following the rules" would guarantee success and meaning in life, it does not and cannot. All that wisdom can do is maximize our potential for a happy life and point us toward faith as the deepest source of meaning and purpose for our lives.

Can Work and Wealth Provide Meaning?

One frequent strategy people use to find meaning and purpose in their lives is work and overwork. We have a term for this strategy: workaholism. The workaholic is addicted to work as a means to achieve meaning in life, and in the process, avoids deep human

---

3. Soren Kierkegaard describes four modes of existence, the Aesthetic, the Ethical, "Religiousness A," and "Religiousness B." One moves from the Aesthetic stage to the Ethical when the meaninglessness of living simply for pleasure dawns on a person. In Religiousness A, one lives under the impression that knowledge of God can be arrived at through reason alone. This search is ultimately proven fruitless, as it did for the Teacher. Religiousness B comes when one submits to God and a wisdom beyond human comprehension. This is Christianity in which we receive a wisdom that transcends human wisdom—the wisdom of the cross (1 Cor 1:22–25).

relationships. In a culture of workaholism, one of the most challenging lessons of Ecclesiastes has to do with the meaning and value of work.

For the wisdom writers, hard work is important and brings a reward, yet, even among wisdom writers, there is a note of caution: work does not guarantee success or economic security. Proverbs records: "Do not wear yourself out to get rich; do not trust your own cleverness. Cast but a glance at riches, and they are gone, for they will surely sprout wings and fly off to the sky like an eagle" (23:4–5). Work is a necessary part of life, but we cannot rely on our economic achievements to give us meaning and purpose in life.

Financial success as a source for meaning and purpose in life fails on a number of levels. First of all, human beings have never been able to answer successfully the question, "How much is enough?" We always want more. Thus, the Teacher says, "The lover of money will not be satisfied with money; nor the lover of wealth, with gain. This also is vanity" (Eccl 5:10 NRSV).[4]

Financial success and wealth fail as a source of meaning and purpose for a second reason: they cannot provide ultimate meaning for life. In the end, all wealth must be left behind, and someone else will enjoy them. The writer of Ecclesiastes puts the matter this way: "As they came from their mother's womb, so they shall go again, naked as they came; they shall take nothing for their toil, which they may carry away with their hands" (v. 15 NRSV). All we possess and all we accomplish upon this earth must ultimately be left behind. It cannot serve as a stable source of meaning and purpose.

Even on this earth, time and chance can result in the loss of wealth and the results of any human accomplishment. The Teacher writes, "I have seen a grievous evil under the sun: wealth hoarded to the harm of its owner or wealth lost through some misfortune, so

---

4. The insatiable appetite of human beings is a constant refrain in Ecclesiastes. For example, "There was a man all alone; he had neither son nor brother. There was no end to his toil, yet his eyes were not content with his wealth. 'For whom am I toiling,' he asked, 'and why am I depriving myself of enjoyment?' This too is meaningless—a miserable business!" (4:8).

that when he has a son, there is nothing left for him" (Eccl 5:13–14). Wealth comes and goes. The stock market rises and falls. Just as we think we have put away a little bit for our children or grandchildren, there is an economic crisis. The search for financial success cannot provide a stable source of meaning.

Even as we labor, build, and amass wealth, we do not know who will enjoy the wealth we accumulate when we are gone. We can work all our lives creating a business and accumulating wealth and then die and leave it to another person. That person may be wise or foolish and waste all we leave behind. The Teacher writes, "I hated all the things I had toiled for under the sun, because I must leave them to the one who comes after me. And who knows whether that person will be wise or foolish? Yet they will have control over all the fruit of my toil into which I have poured my effort and skill under the sun. This too is meaningless" (2:18–19). Money and material possessions cannot provide meaning for our lives.

Can the Moral Life Supply Meaning and Purpose?

Faced with the fact that seeking wealth, pleasure, and accomplishment cannot supply meaning and purpose to life, what about morality? Perhaps by being a good and moral person, what the Jews would have called "righteous," we can achieve meaning and purpose for our lives. One would expect this to be true based upon the constant refrain in the Old Testament that following the Torah, the instructions of God, are key to personal and national success.

The teacher is not so sure. His experience of life, like ours, casts doubt upon the easy assurance of a moral universe that blesses the righteous and punishes the wicked. "In this meaningless life of mine, I have seen both of these: a righteous man perishing in his righteousness and a wicked man living long in his wickedness" (7:15). Righteousness is not a certain path to a meaningful life. Life is complex. Sometimes the wicked are punished. Sometimes justice is defeated, and the righteous receive what the wicked deserve. The Teacher writes, "There is something else meaningless that occurs on earth: the righteous who get what the wicked deserve, and the wicked who get what the righteous deserve. This too, I say, is meaningless" (8:14). Morality is important. But it does not guarantee success or meaning or purpose for living.

The Teacher recognizes that there is a kind of twistedness in human character that makes a moral universe almost impossible. Human beings are "full of evil, and madness is in their hearts while they live, and after that they go to the dead" (9:3 ESV). The Teacher understands what most human beings understand: no human being achieves complete righteousness. Experience teaches that human beings are created upright, but all go astray because of the many schemes by which we attempt to gain what we desire at the expense of others (Eccl 7:29). Even devout, moral people fail and fall short, causing suffering. No matter how good we are, sooner or later we fall short of the righteousness we sense we should achieve and which might provide some source of meaning for our lives.

The limitations and problems of human existence render it impossible to find meaning and purpose in either wisdom or obedience to the moral law. The Teacher concludes:

> So I reflected on all this and concluded that the righteous and the wise and what they do are in God's hands, but no one knows whether love or hate awaits them. All share a common destiny—the righteous and the wicked, the good and the bad, the clean and the unclean, those who offer sacrifices and those who do not. As it is with the good, so with the sinful; as it is with those who take oaths, so with those who are afraid to take them. This is the evil in everything that happens under the sun: The same destiny overtakes all. The hearts of people, moreover, are full of evil and there is madness in their hearts while they live, and afterward they join the dead. (9:1–4)

If we human beings are going to find meaning and purpose in life, we cannot find it solely through the search for wisdom or righteousness.

Accepting Our Common Destiny

The writers of wisdom literature were interested in reality—in the way things are—and in responding to that reality wisely in everyday life. If they had avoided the problems their approach implied, or failed to address its difficulties, they would have been untrue to the very task they posed for themselves: "How can human beings achieve happiness and wholeness in the dangerous business of life?" Therefore, it comes as no surprise that wisdom writers pondered the limitations of their endeavor.

In the end, all the strategies of the wisdom school of Israel fall short. They do not account for the limitations of human existence or the misfortune that so often falls alike upon the righteous and unrighteous, the wise and the foolish. For one thing, all human beings—wise, foolish, good, evil, righteous or not—come to the same end. We all die. Our finite human attempts to create meaning are bound to fail.

While we are alive, we delude ourselves into thinking that the meaningless of life and its lack of ultimate purpose may finally be redeemed by some act of ours, but, in the end, we all die. Worse, because of our self-consciousness, we human beings know that we will one day die, and all of our attempts to build a sense of meaning and purpose will end. No matter how hard we work, no matter how much we accomplish, no matter what moral attainments we achieve, we all die; and our accomplishments die with us (9:5; 11:8). The same destiny overtakes every human being. Life ends.

The Place of Wisdom in a Chaotic Universe

Based on the foregoing, what are we to conclude? Is the search for wisdom and righteousness really important if the moral order of the universe is so chaotic? Why seek wisdom if the universe is so complex and unpredictable that no one can understand it? Why seek to be morally upright if the moral order of the universe is so unstable that the good person cannot be sure he or she will not be punished for the crimes of someone who is wicked?

The author of Ecclesiastes does not degenerate into a kind of postmodern nihilism, as some contend. The Teacher understands the world and its uncertainties. The book makes this point over and over again. Yet over and over again, the writer alerts us to his conviction that the chaos and uncertainties of the world and of human life do not leave us without hope for wisdom and guidance in how to live our lives.

Faced with the meaninglessness of so much of life, the author continues to believe in the existence of a personal God who has given the world a physical and moral order. Like all wisdom literature, Ecclesiastes is partially a book of instruction for the young, and so the last chapter begins with the admonition to "Remember your Creator in the days of your youth, before the days of trouble come, and the years approach when you will say, 'I have no pleasure in them'" (12:1). The author does not reject the wisdom tradition. In fact, the author ends up supporting the need for wise living.

Ecclesiastes ends by restating the fundamental precept of the wise life: respect for God is the beginning of wisdom and of the wise life.

> The end of the matter; all has been heard. Fear God, and keep his commandments; for that is the whole duty of everyone. For God will bring every deed into judgment, including every secret thing, whether good or evil. (12:13–14 NRSV)

The fear of the Lord is the beginning of the wise life, and that foundational principle remains operational despite the fragile and uncertain nature of life. Over and over again, the wisdom writers remind us that humility, remembering who we are and our frailties and failures, is the beginning of wisdom. Without reverence for God and an appreciation of our limitations, we can make no progress in the life of faith, or in the life of wisdom.

A second principle of the wise life that the Teacher upholds is the importance of what might be called "situational awareness." All times are not the same and the wise life involves understanding the times and what is possible given the time. In the most quoted and lovely passage of Ecclesiastes, the author says:

> There is a time for everything, and a season for every activity under heaven: a time to be born and a time to die, a time to plant and a time to uproot, a time to kill and a time to heal, a time to tear down and a time to build, a time to weep and a time to laugh, a time to mourn and a time to dance, a time to scatter stones and a time to gather them, a time to embrace and a time to refrain from embracing, a time to search and a time to give up, a time to keep and a time to throw away, a time to tear and a time to mend, a time to be silent and a time to speak, a time to love and a time to hate, a time for war and a time for peace. (3:1–8)

There can be no formula for the wise life. The wise person must take what can be learned and the principles of wisdom and apply them in an ever changing and always uncertain world.

In the face of the meaningless void of death, the writer of Ecclesiastes cannot provide any ultimate hope. What the writer does do is respond to the ultimate meaningless of life with an understanding that, despite the lack of any ultimate hope for human existence, wisdom is better than folly (2:13; 9:13). Wisdom is better than the passing strength of strong people (9:16). It is better than the victory of armies (v. 17). In the end, wisdom is justified not because it provides meaning and purpose in life or assures happiness. It is simply better than the alternatives.

Ecclesiastes reminds us of the importance of the simple things of life. The pleasures of ordinary life are important, even if they are not ultimately important. We find happiness in living wisely, working hard, enjoying the food we eat, caring for our families, building friendships, and the like. These things are an essential part of a well-lived life. They cannot by themselves give our lives meaning, but they provide happiness and pleasure, fleeting though it may be.

The Postmodern Search for Meaning

There is no book of the Bible more reflective of the postmodern condition than Ecclesiastes. The book deeply respects and reflects the cynical exhaustion of our society—a society that has lost its sense that its fundamental values are sound and they lead to a fuller, meaningful life. The Teacher examines every false god of the Modern Age: workaholism, over-intellectualism, unbalanced moral striving, materialism, pleasure seeking, and the like. In the end, they are all lacking. In contrast to postmodernism, the writer of Ecclesiastes remains grounded by faith in God and in the wisdom tradition. He understands, as postmodern people often do not, that when all is said, the wise, prudent, good life is still to be preferred over a life of wasted energy, moral laxity, over-consumption, and moral and personal dissipation.

Yet, as we shall see, Christianity provides additional reasons for confidence in the wise life. As the writers of the New Testament examined the life of Jesus of Nazareth, they found there a revelation, a new Word from God. This revelation was a revelation of wisdom lived out in self-giving love, of service as the key to an abundant life, of self-denial as a way to self-fulfillment. In the resurrection, they saw God's vindication of the power of goodness and self-giving love to overcome evil even in weakness.

Questions for Reflection

1. In what ways, short of faith have you tried to find meaning and purpose in life? Did they work?

2. The Teacher attempts to find meaning and purpose for his life in success, in building projects, in work. None of it works. Why?

3. When some people are asked why they think they will receive eternal life, they answer, "I have been a good person." One of the Teacher's strategies toward finding meaning and purpose is that of "being a good person." Do you think that being a righteous person can give a person meaning?

4. In the end, the author continues to believe in wisdom and in wise and virtuous living, not because of its ultimate worth, but because it is better than the alternative. Does his solution appeal to you?

Why do you pursue me as God does? Will you never get enough of my flesh? Oh, that my words were recorded, that they were written on a scroll, that they were inscribed with an iron tool on lead, or engraved in rock forever! I know that my redeemer lives, and that in the end he will stand on the earth. And after my skin has been destroyed, yet in my flesh I will see God; I myself will see him with my own eyes—I, and not another. How my heart yearns within me!

JOB 19:22–27

13

The Problem of Suffering

A few years after her death, a biography of Mother Teresa was written. It turns out that Mother Teresa suffered what St. John of the Cross called, "a dark night of the soul." For years, she toiled selflessly, sharing the love of God with forgotten people all over the world. She was unbelievably dedicated and effective at her ministry. Nevertheless, she often felt deserted by God and overcome with despair. If Mother Teresa could suffer in such a way, what hope is there for the rest of us? How can we trust a God who would permit one of his greatest servants to suffer a dark night in which God seemed so absent?[1]

There is no greater threat to faith than the reality of underserved suffering. If human life is ultimately chaotic, and if we can never know from one moment to the next what will happen to us, how can we have faith? Why should we discipline our actions to the stern demands of prudence if anything can happen? Why should we be good if there is no necessary reward for goodness? The wisdom writers did not flinch from these questions and from examining the problems posed by human suffering.

1. Singer, "Letters Reveal Mother Teresa's Secret."

The Problem of Undeserved Suffering

If the problem of Ecclesiastes is the infinite scope of human desire confronting the reality of finitude and the inescapable injustice life brings, Job focuses with laser-like clarity on the problem of undeserved, disproportionate suffering. The question with which Job wrestles is one of the most important in human life: "How can the Way of Wisdom be justified in the face of so much suffering?"

No one knows when Job was written or by whom. The book is based on an old legend of a righteous man named "Job," who experiences unspeakable and undeserved suffering. The legend of Job is recounted in the beginning and end of the book. In between, there are a series of poetic speeches by Job and his friends, as they attempt to understand and explain the cause of his suffering. Job experiences every possible kind of physical, emotional, and spiritual suffering a human being can endure. His children die in a natural disaster. His health is taken from him. His wife and friends desert him. To make matters worse, this suffering is undeserved.

Jane, a mother of several young children, recently contracted an incurable disease. Naturally, her Sunday school class has been praying for her healing. For a time, the cancer went into remission. Unfortunately, the remission was only temporary. The disease returned, and there was little that the doctors could do. All this time, her well-meaning Christian friends continued to diligently pray for her. Eventually they began to wonder why their prayers were not answered as they desired. Finally, they came to the conclusion that it must be that there was some unconfessed sin in Jane's life preventing God from answering their prayers. Of course Jane confessed every sin she could imagine, but there was still no healing. Her prayer partners were unsatisfied, until finally a more mature Christian friend stepped in to assure the young mother that her suffering might have nothing to do with sin, and her lack of healing certainly could not be related to any failure to repent. How could well-meaning Christians be so insensitive? A partial answer is that we, like the wise men of old, want a predictable universe.

The book of Job begins by introducing us to the figure of Job who lived in the land of "Uz," a place we cannot identify except that it is not part of Israel and may be found to the east of the Jordan River. Job is described as blameless and upright, fearing God and shunning evil (Job 1:1). Job was also a blessed person, wealthy beyond imagination, and the father of seven sons and three daughters, a perfect family. (Seven and three are perfect numbers in Hebrew numerology.) He is portrayed as the greatest, most righteous, and wealthiest person of his day (vv. 2–3). Job was also highly religious. So concerned was Job to fulfill his obligations to God that he saw that his children were ritually pure, and he performed sacrifices on their behalf (vv. 4–5). So far as it is possible to describe a human being as righteous before God, Job was such a man.

As the book unfolds, we do not have to take the narrator's word for Job's righteousness: God himself testifies to Job's blameless character. When Satan appears before God, just back from roaming to and fro upon the earth, God asks the accuser, "Have you considered my servant Job? There is no one on earth like him; he is blameless and upright, a man who fears God and shuns evil" (v. 8). Even after God allows Satan to take from him both riches and family, God continues to testify as to Job's moral righteousness, again repeating the refrain, "Have you considered my servant Job? There is no one on earth like him; he is blameless and upright, a man who fears God and shuns evil. And he still maintains his integrity, though you incited me against him to ruin him without any reason" (Job 2:3).

These two affirmations of God are important for understanding the book that bears Job's name. The reader knows from the beginning that Job is a righteous man—so righteous that there is no one on earth like him. If ever a person deserved the blessings of God, it is Job. Any attempt to blame Job for his sufferings is wrong-headed, for

God himself has declared him just. There is yet another reason the reader knows that Job's suffering is undeserved: the reader, unlike Job's friends, is privy to the actual reason for Job's sufferings—reasons having nothing to do with any lack of righteousness of Job or a sin he may have committed. Job is suffering because of a wager between Satan and God.

It is important that, before Job's friends begin speaking, a reader knows that the reason Job is suffering has to do with a wager between Satan and God. Job is not a terrible sinner. In fact, he is more righteous than any person of his day. Job is not irreligious. In fact Job is more religious than any person of his day. Satan has accused Job, bringing against him the only accusation that might hold any water, that Job is righteous only because of the blessings it brings him:

> "Does Job fear God for nothing?" Satan replied. "Have you not put a hedge around him and his household and everything he has? You have blessed the work of his hands, so that his flocks and herds are spread throughout the land. But now stretch out your hand and strike everything he has, and he will surely curse you to your face." (1:9–11)

In the accuser's view, Job will curse God if only God removes his blessing from Job. Job is wise, righteous, and religious for one reason and one reason only—it pays. If it did not pay, Job would deny God just like anyone else. Consequently, God allows the accuser to strike Job and his family.

When the initial loss of family and fortune does not cause Job to lose faith, Satan complains that, although Job has maintained his faithfulness in the face of financial and personal loss, he will certainly deny God if his health and strength are denied him (2:4–5). Therefore, God allows Satan to strike Job's physical body, leaving Job with painful sores—sores so painful and irritating that he must scrape his skin with a broken piece of pottery (vv. 6–8). Even when his wife deserts him, recommending that he curse God and die, Job remains faithful (v. 9).

By the time the introduction is over, the reader knows that Job's suffering is completely undeserved. *The book is about undeserved punishment and affliction.* Any attempt to explain Job's sufferings on the basis of justice must fail, for Job is righteous and his sufferings are undeserved. In other words, the book of Job is about a problem with the traditional wisdom view of life. Over and over again, the wisdom writers assured their pupils that the righteous will prosper and the wicked will suffer. For example, "The name of the righteous is used in blessings, but the name of the wicked will rot" (Prov 10:7). Unfortunately, life presents every believer with a problem: often the wicked do not suffer and the righteous do for what seems to be no good reason at all.

Is All Suffering Deserved?

Ancient Jewish wise men and women were not unrealistic romantics. They saw that life was often unjust, and they were as aware of the injustice and meaningless of much human suffering as any modern cynic. Therefore, they asked the question, "Why?" "Why would a righteous and holy God permit innocent people to suffer undeserved harm?" The book of Job is the vehicle through which Israel, and contemporary people, can think about this dimension of human life and its challenges to faith.

As previously mentioned, the simple moral equation often presented in wisdom literature holds that those who follow the path of wisdom and righteousness will be blessed by God, and those who follow the path of foolishness and wickedness will be cursed. The logical deduction from this worldview is simple: in some way, those who suffer must have brought that suffering upon themselves by their own foolishness or evil.

Job's three friends hold this worldview. Before we criticize these friends too much, let us remember that they were there for Job from the beginning of his suffering. Hearing of his misfortune, they came to be with him for seven days and seven nights. Seven and three being perfect numbers in Jewish numerology, we might see in his friends a perfect attempt to console a sufferer. The fact that they sat silently before the destitute and deformed figure of their friend also speaks well of them. They tried as best they knew to comfort and console. They did not begin with a series of sermons on sin and its consequences.

Ultimately, Job begins to curse the day of his birth. He wishes he had never been born, and he bemoans his fate.

> Why is life given to a man whose way is hidden, whom God has hedged in? For sighing has become my daily food; my groans pour out like water. What I feared has come upon me; what I dreaded has happened to me. I have no peace, no quietness; I have no rest, but only turmoil. (Job 3:23–26)

In this passage Job speaks for every person in human history who has suffered unfairly. He presents the deepest and most unanswerable question and problem of life to his friends, which they (wisely or not) try to answer.

Faced with Job's complaint, Eliphaz, his good friend, feels compelled to defend the moral order of the universe. This begins a series of disputations between Job and his friends. Eliphaz begins by respectfully reminding Job of his past support for the moral order. "Think how you have instructed many, how you have strengthened feeble hands" (4:3). It is as if Eliphaz is gently trying to steer Job away from his anger at God and toward the consolation of wisdom by reminding Job of better days and of his own defense of the moral order of the universe in better times.

Not surprisingly, Eliphaz defends the traditional view that suffering is deserved:

> Consider now: Who, being innocent, has ever perished? Where were the upright ever destroyed? As I have observed, those who plow evil and those who sow trouble reap it. At the breath of God they perish; at the blast of his anger they are no more. (vv. 7–9)

His friend is reminding Job of the moral order of the universe, but Job will have none of it. In his own mind, Job is convinced of his righteousness.

When Eliphaz finishes his speech, Job returns to his complaint. "The arrows of the Almighty are in me; my spirit drinks their poison" (Job 6:4). Job goes on to state his desire to die—then God would have spoken a word of consolation by his death (vv. 8–10). Job refuses to be silent and accept his fate; he continues to cry out in bitterness against it—just as we and our friends do when we suffer without reasons we can understand.

Now, Bildad, his second friend, speaks. He too must defend God against Job's accusations. It is unthinkable that God would act unjustly (Job 8:3). If Job's family has been destroyed, they must have deserved it (v. 4). If Job is innocent as he claims to be, then all he needs to do is pray, and God will restore him (vv. 5–7).[2] Bildad seems to be trying to correct Job while at the same time giving him hope of restoration. In other words, he is being kind.

Job responds that he knows all this and does not need to be reminded by friends of what he already knows (Job 9:2). He is aware of the wisdom and power of God and does not need to be reminded of them. Nor does Job need to be reminded of God's righteousness (vv. 5–20). Job understands that God is just. His plea is personal— God has given Job life and been kind to him (Job 10:12). Job wants comfort from God and a reason for his suffering (vv. 20–22). It is as if Job is speaking for the entire wisdom school of the ancient Near East, reminding them that he is one of them and understands their teachings. Unfortunately, the teachings of the wise just don't help when you are the one suffering!

Zohar, the final friend to speak, is upset with Job. Job seems to assume that a mere human can complain before God, and Zohar disagrees. Job is human and to be human is to be a sinner (Job 11:6).

2. It is important to remember that this is exactly what does happen at the end of the book, so that Job's friend is not so much wrong in his advice as in his assumptions about Job and his family and the cause of their suffering.

Therefore, Zohar believes that Job does not have any complaint against God. He thinks the best thing Job can do is to repent of his sin and ask God for mercy (vv. 13–15).

This is a good place to stop and evaluate the message of the book as it relates to undeserved suffering. Although Job's friends defend the traditional view, Job cannot agree. We, the readers, know that Job's friends are not correct in this case. The fact is that Job is righteous and his suffering cannot be explained on the basis of his sinfulness. The book is constructed in such a way that the limitations of the traditional answer of the wisdom teachers to the problem of evil can be clearly seen.

Job does not deny the power of the traditional view to explain much suffering. In fact, from time to time in the book, Job defends the wisdom tradition. The traditional view is not so much wrong as it is incomplete. It cannot explain the suffering of Job, and by extension the suffering of others like him. *Good people sometimes do suffer, and that suffering cannot always be explained on the basis of sin.* If there is a reason for the suffering of Job, that reason cannot be God's divine justice, for there is no justice that requires the suffering of Job.

Is Suffering a Matter of Divine Discipline?

As a part of his first speech, Eliphaz opens up a second line of argument. Suffering can be explained as discipline. "Blessed is the man whom God corrects, so do not despise the discipline of the Almighty" (Job 5:17), he says. Human beings are like children. Children are often disciplined under circumstances in which they cannot understand the justice of their parents. The wise person accepts discipline of God. It is part of the way human beings acquire wisdom. Once again, this teaching is clearly part of the wisdom tradition. Proverbs teaches, "My son, do not despise the Lord's discipline, and do not resent his rebuke, because the Lord disciplines those he loves, as a father the son he delights in" (3:11–12).

Job cannot accept this reason for his suffering, and neither can the reader. Job is the most righteous person on earth! God has declared him to be so. Job is not a person who needs discipline. He is already wise and righteous. Besides, the reader knows that Job is not being disciplined in this case. He is the victim of some kind of divine wager—his suffering is ultimately inexplicable on moral grounds.

Later in the book, Elihu, a young friend of the wisdom tradition, returns to this argument. He believes Job's friends have done a poor job of defending God, and he is angry at Job for justifying himself before God instead of submitting to God's justice (32:2–3). Elihu launches into a defense of the moral order of the universe and the justice of God, just as Job's friends have previously done:

> So listen to me, you men of understanding. Far be it from God to do evil, from the Almighty to do wrong. He repays everyone for what they have done; he brings on them what their conduct deserves. It is unthinkable that God would do wrong, that the Almighty would pervert justice. (34:10–12)

If Job is suffering, then he deserves it, for all human beings have sinned.

According to Elihu, the justice of God is absolute because he sees all things, knows all things, and nothing can escape his understanding (32:17–27).[3] For Elihu, Job's greatest sin is his resentment against what God has done and his refusal to repent, accept God's discipline, and be restored (34:33–37). If Job, being at least a relatively righteous person, will only repent and accept this discipline from God, as disproportionate as it seems, God will renew him:

> God is mighty, but despises no one; he is mighty, and firm in his purpose. He does not keep the wicked alive but gives the afflicted their rights. He does not take his eyes off the righteous; he enthrones them with kings and exalts them forever. But if people are bound in chains, held fast by

---

3. This line of argument cannot be used to explain Job's suffering, for we know that the suffering of Job is due to a bet between God and Satan.

cords of affliction, he tells them what they have done—that they have sinned arrogantly. He makes them listen to correction and commands them to repent of their evil. If they obey and serve him, they will spend the rest of their days in prosperity and their years in contentment. (36:5–11)

Once again, though what Elihu says may be true, it is inapplicable. It is true that all men sin and that Job is a sinner. It is true that we are not appropriate judges of the consequences of our sin. It is true that sometimes the suffering of a human being far outweighs our human evaluation of the extent of their sin. However, this does not explain Job's suffering because God himself has proclaimed Job to be just and undeserving of suffering. In the end, Elihu succeeds no better than his elders. The new generation of wisdom thinkers is just as stumped by the problem of suffering as the older generation was.

Does the Majesty of God Explain Suffering?

Many who read Job are unsatisfied with its ending. When the dialogue between Job and his friends is complete, God speaks. In these speeches, God reminds Job that God's wisdom and human wisdom are of a different character:

> Where were you when I laid the earth's foundation? Tell me, if you understand. Who marked off its dimensions? Surely you know! Who stretched a measuring line across it? On what were its footings set, or who laid its cornerstone—while the morning stars sang together and all the angels shouted for joy? (38:4–7)

It is as if the wisdom writers understand that the problem of suffering is a serious one and that their explanations are not adequate. The only logical move they can imagine is to place undeserved suffering within the scope of the mysterious secret wisdom and sovereignty of God.

God's justice cannot be satisfactorily explained by human reason, and it is a mistake to try. During the long speech, God confronts Job with his majestic, transcendent power. Job cannot answer and is silent (40:1-2). After God is finished speaking, Job has his final word—a word of submission to God:

> I know that you can do all things; no purpose of yours can be thwarted. You asked, "Who is this that obscures my plans without knowledge?" Surely I spoke of things I did not understand, things too wonderful for me to know. You said, "Listen now, and I will speak; I will question you, and you shall answer me." My ears had heard of you but now my eyes have seen you. Therefore I despise myself and repent in dust and ashes. (42:2-6)

In the end, we are left in the book of Job, as we are left in human life, with a mystery. We cannot understand undeserved suffering, its causes or its justice.

Does Job Need a Judge or a Redeemer?

There is a theme in Job that provides a clue to unraveling the quandary in which Job leaves us. This clue may also explain why the argument of God satisfies Job though it may not satisfy the modern critic. Time and time again, Job asks for a hearing from God. He wants God to come, hear his complaint, and give him some explanation of his suffering. It is as if Job does not so much want a *reason* for his suffering as a *relationship* with the One who allowed him to suffer.

Job also understands that God is not a human being, and because he (Job) is a human being, he might not be able to survive a confrontation with God (9:1-14). In other words, Job sees a need for some intermediary who can communicate his complaint before God:

> He is not a mere mortal like me that I might answer him, that we might confront each other in court. If only there were someone to mediate between us, someone to bring us

together, someone to remove God's rod from me, so that
his terror would frighten me no more. (vv. 32–34)

In this and in similar passages, Job seems to be struggling for a relationship to God other than mere submission to an almighty and
all-powerful judge.

In the most famous and most quoted section of the book, Job
cries out for a redeemer and expresses his faith that such a God
might be present for him:

Oh, that my words were written! Oh, that they were inscribed in a book! That they were engraved on a rock with
an iron pen and lead, forever. For I know *that* my Redeemer lives, And He shall stand at last on the earth; And after
my skin is destroyed, this *I know,* That in my flesh I shall
see God, Whom I shall see for myself, And my eyes shall
behold, and not another. *How* my heart yearns within me!
(19:23–27 NKJV)

In the midst of suffering and pain, Job sees that there is no adequate
explanation for human suffering unless our human eyes are trans-
ported beyond this world and we see a God who is more than a just
judge—a God who is also a loving redeemer.

The New Testament Resolution

In the New Testament there is a story about a man who is blind from
birth. Jesus' disciples, formed in the culture of the Jewish faith, know
that traditional Jewish teaching requires that suffering have some
explanation in sin. So they ask Jesus, "Who sinned, this man or his
parents that he was born blind?" (John 9:1–2). The disciples pose
the same questions to Jesus that Job poses to God: "Would someone
please explain this suffering to us?"

Jesus does not answer his disciples on the basis of the wisdom
tradition. Instead he says, "Neither this man nor his parents sinned,"
said Jesus, "but this happened so that the works of God might be

displayed in him" (v. 3). It is as if Jesus is turning the question of his disciples into a demonstration of the loving presence of God.

This leads to another way of looking at Job. The wisdom teachers were so focused on the wisdom and the power of God that they did not address the question most modern people have: "If God is a God of love, then how can God allow suffering?" If there is an explanation that we can accept, it will come in the form of a God who suffers with and for us, the God revealed in Jesus, not in rational arguments such as those of Job and his friends. We cannot know the precise cause of anyone's suffering. Having chosen to create a world in which human beings could emerge, God allows nature and human nature to take its course. The result is suffering, much of it undeserved and inexplicable.[4] All the human and natural evils human beings endure are the price the world and all of its people pay for our existence. Suffering is part of life.

Job ends with the problem of human suffering unresolved. His friends have given the traditional answers of the wisdom tradition. None of the answers have satisfactorily explained the problem. In the end, the book resolves the disputes among Job and his friends through an appearance of God in which God himself answers Job. The answer is outside of the wisdom tradition—underserved suffering cannot be explained by any appeal to human reason. It can only be understood as an aspect of the mystery of the All Powerful, All Knowing God of Israel (Job 38–39).

Suffering cannot be explained. It can only be endured with faith. Job does not come to understand this suffering by any exercise of human wisdom. He comes to understand that as a human being he cannot know and is unworthy to know the secret purposes and counsels of God (Job 40:4). Job finally admits to God:

> I know that you can do anything, and no one can stop you. You asked, "Who is this that questions my wisdom with such ignorance?" It is I—and I was talking about things

---

4. See Polkinghorne, *Exploring Reality*, 136–46.

I knew nothing about, things far too wonderful for me.
(42:2–3 NLT)

The answer to the problem of undeserved suffering, if it can be found, cannot be found in the wisdom tradition.

Where, then, is God in our suffering? Perhaps the best explanation is that God is in the midst of it all in Christ, the Word of God, suffering with every sufferer, taking upon himself the guilt and pain of the world, deserved and undeserved. In the words of John Polkinghorne:

> He is not a spectator, but a fellow-sufferer, who has himself absorbed the full force of evil. In the lonely figure hanging in the darkness and dereliction of Calvary, the Christian believes that he sees God opening his arms to embrace the bitterness of the strange world he has made. The God revealed in the vulnerability of the incarnation and in the vulnerability of creation are one. He is the crucified God, whose paradoxical power is perfected in weakness, whose self-chosen symbol is the King reigning from the gallows.[5]

On the cross we see revealed the truth that God not only reigns in glory over his creation, but paradoxically, suffers the travail of its finitude, incompleteness, brokenness, sin, and suffering. In the end, the wisdom tradition points beyond itself to One greater than the tradition. Christians believe that the One Greater than Wisdom— One greater than Solomon—did come and in his coming moves our thinking and understanding to a new level. God does not stand outside our human suffering. Instead, through his personal appearance in Christ, God is a fellow sufferer with each human being.

5. Polkinghorne, *Science and Providence*, 79.

Questions for Reflection

1. Have you ever experienced undeserved suffering? What was it like? What were your feelings?

2. Do you feel that it helps you or anyone else to feel that the suffering was deserved? Why or why not?

3. During a time in which you were suffering, did your faith grow or suffer as a result of suffering? How so?

4. Job ends with Job repenting in the face of the power and majesty of God. Is this solution acceptable to you?

As I looked, thrones were set in place,
and the Ancient of Days took his seat.
His clothing was as white as snow;
the hair of his head was white like wool.
His throne was flaming with fire,
and its wheels were all ablaze.
A river of fire was flowing,
coming out from before him.
Thousands upon thousands attended him;
ten thousand times ten thousand stood before him.
The court was seated, and the books were opened.

DANIEL 7:9–10

14

The End of Understanding

There is no area of the Bible more prone to misinterpretation than those books we call "apocalyptic."[1] When my wife and I were first married, a well-known local preacher announced that the end of the world was likely to be Easter Sunday of that year. At the time, she was sitting in a hospital bed holding our first child who had just been born. She was filled with sadness and regret because, if this were correct, our child would only live a few months. Remembering Jesus' teaching that "no one knows the day or the hour" she quickly recovered her composure. History soon proved this preacher mistaken. It would seem that his teaching that day was both wrong-headed and irrelevant to anyone who wanted wisdom for daily living.

Nowhere do "practical" or "realistic" people have more trouble interpreting the Bible than in the area of apocalyptic literature and the often overly literalistic way in which preachers use such literature. Wisdom involves acting shrewdly in the events of day-to-day life with a view towards one's ultimate happiness. What can visions of the future filled with obscure metaphors, mystical beasts, and the like have to do with gaining wisdom and meeting day-to-day needs to face the challenges of life? *The answer is that extraordinary times*

---

1. This section only deals with Daniel and not with other Old and New Testament eschatological books. Its approach is applicable to any eschatological book or passage.

require extraordinary wisdom. Times of stress and persecution place pressure on men and women to lose faith because of the seeming hopelessness of a current situation. Sometimes, human beings are called to maintain integrity under circumstances of danger, persecution, opposition, and stress. In such times, we need a kind of wisdom and encouragement different from that required in ordinary times. In difficult and dangerous times, we need assurance that God is and will be with us. We need assurance that our suffering is not without meaning and will end in due time. We need to have an assurance that our suffering is part of a story bigger than our own lives and in which our lives and our suffering make perfect sense.

Daniel is one of the most-studied and controversial books in the Bible. There are many aspects to the book, and it is critically important to have some understanding of the period between the Babylonian captivity of the Jews and the approaching New Testament period. The book is divided into two parts. Chapters 1–6 are stories taken from the life of Daniel and his friends. These stories reflect Daniel's life from the period between Daniel's arrival in Babylon under the reign of Nebuchadnezzar (605 BC) and the time of Cyrus the Great, or about the year 531 BC—a period of about seventy years. The timing and character of the stories imply that Daniel lived approximately from the final defeat of Judah around the year 587 BC until shortly after the decree of Cyrus that allowed the Jews to return to the Holy Land about seventy years later. Thus, his active life of public service spanned the Neo-Babylonian and Medo-Persian periods.[2]

Faithfulness in a Foreign Place

The first part of Daniel contains a series of stories about the character and life of Daniel and his three friends, Shadrach, Meshach, and

2. As with most, if not all, controversial areas of Scripture, scholars do not agree as to the historicity of the stories of Daniel's life nor do they agree concerning the time periods during which the book was written. For the purposes of this book, these scholarly disputes are not important.

Abednego, after they are transplanted from their home in Judah to the court of the Neo-Babylonian kings. These stories reflect the blessings one can expect from faithfulness to the law of God (Dan 1–2), maintaining faith when trials and tests come because that power is fallen, evil, or insane (Dan 3), and the value of speaking the truth to power despite the cost (Dan 3, 5, 6). These vignettes teach the virtue of faithful service to God even when under cultural and other pressures to conform to behaviors and standards that faith rejects. In these stories, Daniel is portrayed as able to maintain his faith and integrity in the midst of the trials and challenges confronting a captive people. These stories have enduring worth as encouragement for men and women of faith to hold fast to their faith even when, as is often the case in our society, they are under overt or covert pressure to conform to a pagan society.

Faithfulness in the Face of Persecution

The second part of the book begins in chapter 7 with a dream Daniel has of four beasts. This dream recalls a dream of Nebuchadnezzar in chapter 2 that sets out the kingdoms of the world from the Neo-Babylonian Empire until the rise of Rome as a world power. In this section of the book, we are introduced to "the Ancient of Days" (Dan 7:9) and "one like a son of man" (v. 13), who receives the power and the authority of the Ancient of Days and is given an everlasting dominion, which kingdom cannot be destroyed (v. 14). Christians have always seen the risen Christ in this vision.

The first of Daniel's visions is dated during the reign of Belshazzar, whom Daniel earlier confronted with his mortality and with the mortality of the Neo-Babylonian Empire (Dan 5). In this dream, Daniel sees four beasts rising up out of the chaos of the sea of human history (7:3). The first beast is like a lion, with the body of a lion and wings like an eagle. Though it is a beast, it is given a heart like a human being (v. 4). The second beast looks like a bear raised up on one side, and it is eating three ribs (v. 5). The third beast is like a four-headed leopard with wings like a bird (v. 6). The final beast is unlike any animal with which humans are familiar. This terrible beast eats and tramples underfoot whatever it touches (v. 7).

Many commentators coordinate this dream with an earlier dream of Nebuchadnezzar in which the king sees a statue with a head of gold, chests and arms of silver, loins and thighs of bronze, and feet of iron and clay (Dan 2:31–33). These commentators see the kingdoms of the two dreams as representing the kingdoms of the world from the time of Nebuchadnezzar until the Roman Empire. The exact identity of the kingdoms, however, may not matter as much as their representation of a long chain of kingdoms of this world formed by war, conquest, and violence. These sorts of kingdoms and powers still exist in our day.

Chapter 8 contains a vision of a two-horned ram and a one-horned he-goat. In the case of this dream, we are given an interpretation that identifies the ram with the Medo-Persian Empire and the he-goat with the empire of Alexander the Great (v. 9–22). When the horn of Alexander is broken off at the height of its power, four horns emerge (v. 8). As a matter of historical fact, at the death of Alexander the Great, his kingdom was divided among four of his generals: Cassander, Lysimachus, Ptolemy, and Seleucius. During this vision of beasts, we are introduced to another horn that becomes great for a season (v. 9). This horn is usually identified with Antiochus Epiphanes IV, a descendant of Selucius who ruled from about 175 to 164 BC. Antioches Epiphanes IV persecuted the Jews in a terrible way. Daniel 11 contains a detailed symbolic account of the rule of Antiochus.

Taken as a whole, these visions represent the unstable history of the ancient Middle East from the time of Nebuchadnezzar, through empires of Cyrus of Persia, Alexander the Great, and the kings of the Hellenistic era, to the time of the emergence of Rome as a world power. It is a story of war, conquest, and persecution. In the words of Macbeth, "It is a tale told by an idiot, full of sound and fury, signifying nothing."[3] The question for believers is: "What meaning can we find in this tale of madness, greed, and conquest?"

God's Sovereign Power Over History

In chapter 9, Daniel prays to God one of the great prayers of the Old Testament and is visited by an angelic figure. In chapter 10, Daniel has a vision of a man dressed in linen with fiery eyes and a voice like a multitude (vv. 5–6). Earlier, Daniel is given a vision of "the Ancient of Days"—God on his throne in heaven itself:

> As I looked, thrones were set in place, and the Ancient of Days took his seat. His clothing was as white as snow; the hair of his head was white like wool. His throne was flaming with fire, and its wheels were all ablaze. A river of fire was flowing, coming out from before him. Thousands upon thousands attended him; ten thousand times ten thousand stood before him. The court was seated, and the books were opened. (Dan 7:9–10)

This vision is of the all-powerful, sovereign God of history before whose eyes all the secrets of history stand open and whose power is available to protect his people. Within the vision of God on his throne we are introduced to another figure ("one like a son of man") who is given authority, glory, and sovereign power over all peoples and nations—one whose kingdom will never end, pass away, or be destroyed (vv. 13–14).

The Nature of Apocalyptic Literature

The visions of Daniel represent a kind of literature called "apocalyptic," derived from a Greek word that means "to unveil." It is as if the future, which is normally hidden from our eyes, is suddenly revealed. Of course, we human beings cannot precisely know the future. It is

3. Shakespeare, *MacBeth*, act 5, scene 5.

hidden from our eyes, bounded as we are by time and space in all of our knowing. Therefore, the language of apocalyptic literature is metaphorical and symbolic. Rather than primarily giving detailed information about the future, apocalyptic literature affords hope to sustain faith during an uncertain present while giving us highly symbolic information concerning future events.

Because human beings cannot know the future, apocalypse descriptions should not be taken literally, if by "literally" we mean as a detailed description of the future or the course of current events. Instead, apocalyptic writings primarily reveal what people of faith need to understand about the future in order to be faithful in loving God and others, knowing that in the end, God will make things right.

In apocalyptic literature, human reason reaches a boundary beyond which it cannot go. Human beings cannot see the future. We cannot observe and know the precise purposes in human history of the invisible God who exists beyond the boundaries of time and space. We cannot be sure of the outcome of the challenges and events of our own time. When human reason reaches its limits, the stage is set for religious vision and experience.

In apocalyptic visions, indeed in any kind of religious vision, believers reach the boundary of human understanding and come into direct contact with God.[4] In a vision, our normal conceptual tools are still operating, but no longer in their accustomed manner and context. The result is a "breaking through" in images, dreams, visions, and metaphors. Earthly objects may be present, but they are transformed—there are lions with wings of eagles, rams that fly over the ground with a speed that is astounding, leopards that have wings. The message is mostly disclosed by God through dreams or visions or by angelic messengers. These and other images are used to convey information that is normally unavailable to human beings. There is most often a simple and clear message amidst the symbols of apocalyptic literature—God's will triumphs in the end. Love wins in

4. See Polanyi, *Personal Knowledge*, 196–97, for a more theoretical explanation of this phenomenon.

the end. Truth wins in the end. Justice will eventually triumph over injustice.

There are important things to remember about apocalyptic literature if we want to gain wisdom from it. Apocalyptic passages are normally written in times of oppression, persecution, uncertainty, danger, and challenge to people of faith. Because of the circumstances that give rise to apocalyptic writings, they frequently depict in concrete language the eternal battle between good and evil, a battle being fought both on earth in human history and in heaven among the angels. Because these writings represent both concrete and spiritual events in circumstances involving danger, apocalyptic writings are written in poetic and/or figurative language. They refer to current events in veiled and symbolic ways.

Apocalyptic writings are designed to encourage downtrodden people. They provide hope that God will intervene in the events of human history to bring evil to judgment, to achieve ultimate victory over human sin, and to rescue the people of God from their current circumstances. In apocalyptic literature, we learn that, however uncertain our future may be, our suffering and sacrifice will be redeemed by God. In this way, apocalyptic writings are designed to bring hope to people of faith in difficult times. Therefore, apocalyptic literature is not just for a few academics who have special skills to decode the mystery or for special people who study the writings deeply. They are for the entire people of God.[5]

Penny is fourteen years old. She has just returned from a Bible study led by an older girl from her church. She does not want to go back. For the past several weeks, Penny and a group of girls have been studying Revelation. The leader of the little Bible study is a high school friend of the family who is learning to teach the Bible. She has been giving the girls a

---

5. This short explanation of the nature of apocalyptic literature is based on a summary prepared by Rev. Dr. Cindy Schwartz for a sermon on the book of Daniel. See Schwartz, "In the End."

very literal explanation of the book, including her belief that a time of suffering is near for believers. Penny has been having nightmares. She knows she will have nightmares tonight. Her mother is friends with the mother of the leader, so she is somewhat reluctant to tell her mother how scared and worried she is. For Penny this Bible study is a turning point: She will never enjoy Bible studies or prayer groups with her friends again. They will always bring bad memories.

Apocalyptic Literature as Wisdom Literature

Apocalyptic literature is a type of wisdom literature: it involves the search for wisdom taken to its limits—to a vision of the end of human history or the end of some period of human history. God, in his mercy and grace, reveals that part of the end of history that believers need to know to live faithfully—not every detail of the future, but all we need to know to act as his people and representatives on earth. In so doing, apocalyptic literature provides an explanation of the present that allows faith to confront and live into an uncertain future.

As mentioned earlier, a characteristic of human beings is that we tend to live our lives as if we were characters in a story. In order to make sense of our lives and act wisely in the midst of history, human beings need some idea of where history is heading and how the story ends. Apocalyptic revelation provides the glimpse of history and its final meaning we need in order to play our part in God's unfolding story.

There is always a temptation in reading apocalyptic literature to attempt to establish a one-to-one correspondence between the vision, dream, or other revelation and events in our own time or in the future of the world. Historically, this is sometimes possible since the writers of apocalyptic literature were often trying to convey precise information to a group of believers. Often, however, the visions have multiple meanings for believers at the time and, metaphorically, to believers of all time. As to the future applicability of such literature, it is best to remember the words of Jesus: no one knows the day or the hour (Matt 24:36). The importance of apocalyptic literature is not in the specifics of the future, but in imparting the wisdom to react appropriately to it.

Fundamentally, apocalyptic literature provides God's assurance that there is an order and purpose to human history and our lives. History is not chaotic or senseless. Our lives are not "sound and fury signifying nothing." God is in control of the circumstances and events of our lives. God's loving purpose in history will prevail, not through violence and conquest as with earthly kingdoms, but through the slow process of love and wisdom working for truth, goodness, beauty, and justice. This gives us the courage to continue living wisely and with love toward God and others, even in times of dislocation, unrest, and persecution.

Modern people too often study apocalyptic literature looking for a systematic correlation between its transcendent content and contemporary events: the locust in Revelation must be military helicopters and the like. This kind of interpretation misses the point. Apocalyptic literature is by its nature symbolic, and the symbols, whatever substance they may have had for the original readers, point to the same moral and spiritual conclusions as were intended for those who first read the books.

Whenever we reduce an apocalyptic passage to a simple correspondence with a time or person, we collapse the universal meaning of the passage into our personal history. In so doing, we lose the eternal message of the passage—and often make fools of ourselves. Just to give an example, as the American armies were descending on Bagdad in the Second Gulf War, a well-known writer re-published a book identifying Saddam Hussein as the Anti-Christ. I joked with our church members that the book had better sell out before the United States Army reached Bagdad. Events have proven the author wrong. Instead of trying to find in Daniel and other apocalyptic writings a detailed roadmap of the future course of history, we need to find in these writings confidence and hope in every situation. In the end, God wins through love and wisdom. We can too.

The usefulness of apocalyptic literature as wisdom literature and as literature for moral training also remains. The powers and principalities that were at work in the time of Daniel are still at work in our own time. We too face dragons and beasts from the sea. Often, we fail to recognize them; for in our day they frequently wear Brooks Brothers suits. Confronted with the perplexing issues of our time, we sometimes need to hear the words of the angel to Daniel: "As for you, go your way till the end. You will rest, and then at the end of the days you will rise to receive your allotted inheritance" (Dan 12:13). The moral character with which Daniel faces the challenges of the rise and fall of the empires of his day is the same character we need in our own day.

In both the Old and New Testaments believers are confronted by earthly powers that are deeply antagonistic to the people of God. History is full of examples of persecution of Christians and Jews. In such times, it is hard to make sense of the world—and harder still to remain faithful. Only a conviction that God cares for his people, is still active in the sufferings of his people, and intends to redeem the pain of suffering for his people makes the virtues of faith, hope, and love possible. To reduce apocalyptic literature to a kind of comic book roadmap to the future is to ignore the deepest and most important aspect of this kind of literature.

Questions for Reflection

1. When you think of the word "apocalypse" what comes to your mind?

2. Do you agree that in this kind of literature we primarily find wisdom for living in dangerous times with faithfulness and confidence in God? If your answer is, "Yes," what difference does this make for how you apply its teachings in everyday life?

3. What aspects of our world and times do you see reflecting the same forces that shaped the life of Daniel and the book that bears his name?

4. What kind of encouragement do you get from the assurances found in Daniel and in books like Revelation that God is in control and that his will for human history cannot be thwarted?

Surely I am too stupid to be a man. I have not the understanding of a man.I have not learned wisdom, nor have I knowledge of the Holy One.Who has ascended to heaven and come down?Who has gathered the wind in his fists?Who has wrapped up the waters in a garment?Who has established all the ends of the earth?What is his name, and what is his son's name?Surely you know!

PROVERBS 30:2–4 (ESV)

15

One Greater than Wisdom

The End of the Intellectual Search for Wisdom

We have seen that wisdom literature, committed to an unflinching search for truth and an understanding of the reality of human life, squarely faced the problems inherent in a simple equation of blessings, success, and meaning with the wise life. Job, Ecclesiastes, and Daniel, each in its own way, address the reality that good people suffer, much suffering does not make sense, and wisdom does not prevent a wise person from experiencing injustice and meaninglessness inherent to much of human life.

In Job and in Ecclesiastes, one senses the conviction that any explanation of the human condition must finally come as through a personal revelation from God. This is why Job is so insistent that he have a personal interview with God. His friends are not adequate mediators of reasons for his suffering. He wants God to personally hear and answer his case, and by extrapolation every sufferer's case. Somehow, the character of God is at stake in the problems of meaningless and undeserved suffering. To the one who suffers undeservedly or who loses a sense that life has meaning, much of the time God seems strangely silent.

Near the end of Proverbs, there is a passage that speaks of the ultimate helplessness of human reason in the face of the deepest questions of life. It is as if in frustration the wisdom writers finally confess the futility of trying to understand the ways of God:

> I am weary, O God; I am weary and worn out, O God. I am too stupid to be human, and I lack common sense. I have not mastered human wisdom, nor do I know the Holy One. Who but God goes up to heaven and comes back down? Who holds the wind in his fists? Who wraps up the oceans in his cloak? Who has created the whole wide world? What is his name—and his son's name? Tell me if you know! (Prov 30:1–4 NLT)

This passage expresses a fundamental problem with the human search for wisdom: we are not God. We cannot ascend to heaven and check out our earthly conclusions with the Almighty. The search for God and for human wisdom with respect to the most important questions of life ultimately reaches the end of human understanding. More arguments will not suffice—a revelation is needed. One is tempted to quote the modern philosopher Ludwig Wittgenstein, "Whereof one cannot speak, thereof one must be silent."[1]

Human beings must live within the limits of human understanding. Unfortunately, the ways of God are beyond our understanding. If we humans are going to find answers to life's most troubling questions, God must reveal them to us. We cannot ascend to God or investigate God and find our answers. God must come down and communicate with us. In addition, since our deepest need for a sense of the *presence* of God, not simply a word from God, the revelation we need must be *personal* not merely verbal.[2]

---

1. Wittgenstein, *Tractatus Logico-Philosophicus*, 90.

2. This is probably one reason pastors and other caregivers quickly learn that our presence with people who are suffering is far more important than anything we may say. In fact, as Job's friends illustrate, what we say may interfere with the comfort of our presence!

One Greater than Solomon

New Testament writers would agree to this need for personal revelation for a surprising reason: they had seen the mysterious, inscrutable God revealed in human flesh. When they saw Jesus, they saw revealed a kind of wisdom so different from their expectations that it initially seemed foolish. As they reflected on the revelation of Christ, they came to understand it as foundational to any rational understanding of God and of the universe. In Christ the abstract world of wisdom and the concrete world of everyday life had become unified in a single human life. The secret wisdom of God was revealed to the world so that now we can in fact speak intelligently about it.

In Matthew 12, Jesus alludes to his special status. The Scribes and the Pharisees had been challenging Jesus because he seemed not to follow the wisdom of the Jewish tradition as they understood it. Finally, Jesus responds. Here is how Matthew relates the story:

> Then some of the scribes and Pharisees said, "Master, we want to see a sign from you." But Jesus told them, "It is an evil and unfaithful generation that craves for a sign, and no sign will be given to it—except the sign of the prophet Jonah. For just as Jonah was in the belly of that great sea-monster for three days and nights, so will the Son of Man be in the heart of the earth for three days and nights. The men of Nineveh will stand up with this generation in the judgment and will condemn it. For they did repent when Jonah preached to them, and you have more than Jonah's preaching with you now! The Queen of the South will stand up in the judgment with this generation and will condemn it. *For she came from the ends of the earth to listen to the wisdom of Solomon, and you have more than the wisdom of Solomon with you now!*" (Matt 12:38–42 Philips; emphasis added)

The Scribes and the Pharisees wanted a sign that Jesus was an authentic teacher of the wisdom of God that they could fit into their pre-existing worldview. They wanted a Messiah that fit their expectations.

Jesus refused their request, telling them that they would indeed get a sign—but not a sign that they would understand or could accept. Although in Jesus one greater than Solomon is present, they will have to change their expectations in the face of the reality of the Messiah God has sent to them.[3]

The leaders of Israel must have thought to themselves, "This Jesus a greater teacher than Solomon? Who does he think he is?" Who among the teachers of Israel could be a greater teacher of wisdom than the patron saint of the wisdom tradition, the son of David? Here Jesus is making his case that, as "one has come down from heaven," he is the authentic and reliable guide to the wise life. However, this wisdom is not a wisdom the world will easily recognize or accept. In fact, the very people who might have been expected to recognize Jesus as the bearer of true wisdom reject and crucify him. His wisdom will require a complete change of worldview and a complete change of expectations in order to be understood. His wisdom will not be understood except by an act of faith and of trust that the person Jesus is and was reveals the Living God.

The Word Made Flesh

It is not just the spoken words of Jesus that are important. In his very *being*, his presence there is revealed as the Word and Wisdom of God. John begins his gospel:

> In the beginning was the Word, and the Word was with God, and the Word was God. He was with God in the beginning. Through him all things were made; without him nothing was made that has been made. In him was life, and that life was the light of all mankind. The light shines

3. Torrance, *Theological Science*. In scientific, religious, and other thinking there can only be real knowledge when an investigator adjusts his or her view of reality to the nature of the subject matter. "[In] Jesus Christ God has broken into the closed circle of our inability and adequacy, and estrangement and self-will, and within our alien condition has achieved and established real knowledge of Himself" (ibid., 51).

in the darkness, and the darkness has not overcome it. . . .
The Word became flesh and made his dwelling among us.
We have seen his glory, the glory of the one and only Son,
who came from the Father, full of grace and truth. (John
1:1–8, 14)

In Christ, God has chosen to make a personal appearance in human
history. In Jesus, the wisdom that was with the Father in the beginning as a master craftsman of creation (Prov 8) has come to dwell in
human history and is now revealed not just in words but also in a
human being whose character is "full of grace and truth" (John 1:14).

Despite the presence of the True Light of God's wisdom in Jesus,
the True Light was not easy to recognize (v. 9). In fact, "though the
world was made through him, the world did not recognize him" (v.
10). When John says that the world did not receive him, he does not
just mean the gentile nations who might be expected to miss the purpose and meaning of his life. Not even his own people, who had been
prepared for his coming throughout their long history, understood.
"He came to that which was his own, but his own did not receive
him" (v. 11).

The New Testament is replete with indications that Jesus and
his teachings often puzzled even those closest to him, the disciples.[4]
They did not always understand his parables and frequently had to
have them explained to them (Mark 4:13). In Matthew 13, Jesus tells
a series of parables that his followers have difficulty understanding.
Then, the reason is given:

> Jesus spoke all these things to the crowd in parables; he
> did not say anything to them without using a parable. So
> was fulfilled what was spoken through the prophet: "I will
> open my mouth in parables, I will utter things hidden
> since the creation of the world." (vv. 34–35)

4. One of the motifs of the Gospel of Mark is the incomprehension of the
disciples despite their constant contact with Jesus.

Jesus' teachings were difficult to understand and his wisdom often confusing because he revealed a hidden wisdom from God (1 Cor 1:18–19). This wisdom can only be recognized on the basis of the revelation God is making through Jesus received by faith.

The core misunderstanding of the disciples concerned the character of Jesus and of God. Jesus revealed a wisdom that does not necessarily result in wealth, success, or victory. It is not a wisdom that brings with it adulation of crowds or political or economic power. It is not a wisdom that the best and the brightest of the academy will necessarily applaud. It is a wisdom that leads to a cross. It is a wisdom shown by submitting to injustice. In other words, if we possess merely a human wisdom formed by the notion that wisdom brings success and adulation, what Jesus reveals will seem to be no kind of wisdom at all.

The Wisdom of the Cross

The Apostle Paul expresses the surprise the apostles felt at Christ's incomprehensible self-disclosure of God's self-giving wisdom:

> For the message of the cross is foolishness to those who are perishing, but to us who are being saved it is the power of God. For it is written: "I will destroy the wisdom of the wise; the intelligence of the intelligent I will frustrate." Where is the wise person? Where is the teacher of the law? Where is the philosopher of this age? Has not God made foolish the wisdom of the world? For since in the wisdom of God the world through its wisdom did not know him, God was pleased through the foolishness of what was preached to save those who believe. Jews demand signs and Greeks look for wisdom, but we preach Christ crucified: a stumbling block to Jews and foolishness to Gentiles, but to those whom God has called, both Jews and Greeks, Christ the power of God and the wisdom of God. For the foolishness of God is wiser than human wisdom, and the weakness of God is stronger than human strength. (vv. 18–25)

The wisdom Christ revealed is so unimaginable that no form of human understanding could have foreseen its character. The Jews rejected it because it defied their messianic expectations of a military and political deliverer. The Greeks rejected it because their ideas of divinity postulated an impassible God who could not suffer, a God beyond the misery of this world and its bondage to sin, suffering, and death. We will also reject it and consider it foolishness if we attempt to receive it on the basis of our cultural expectations of the nature of wisdom and its results.

The wisdom of God is a paradoxical wisdom, a wisdom that must be accepted by faith before it makes sense. It is a wisdom that no person wise by Jewish or Greek standards would have predicted. It is a wisdom revealed not in strength, but in weakness and in self-giving love. It is a wisdom that does not fit into the categories of thought prevalent in Jesus' day or in our own. It cannot be assimilated into any human wisdom other than by making it the foundation of a new kind of wisdom.[5]

The reality and power of God's wisdom can only be known in the person of the crucified and resurrected Jesus Messiah (1 Cor 2:2). It can only be known in humble reliance upon God's mercy, which is its basis and foundation (v. 3). It cannot be known with the wisest and most persuasive arguments; it can only be known in the experience of personal forgiveness and restoration by the power of the Holy Spirit (vv. 4–5).

This is a wisdom that cannot be known by the rulers and authorities of "this age" because it is a hidden wisdom:

> But we speak God's wisdom, secret and hidden, which God decreed before the ages for our glory. None of the rulers of this age understood this; for if they had, they would not have crucified the Lord of glory. But, as it is written, "What no eye has seen, nor ear heard, nor the human heart conceived, what God has prepared for those who love him"— these things God has revealed to us through the Spirit; for

5. Newbigin, *Foolishness to the Greeks*, 126–27.

the Spirit searches everything, even the depths of God. (vv. 7–10 NRSV)

The ultimate expression of God's hidden wisdom could not be expressed in words. It had to be expressed on a cross and can only be appropriated in a personal relationship with God as revealed on the cross. Those who understand this wisdom must have their mind completely transformed so that they have the mind of Christ, the mind of the One who revealed this wisdom, this hidden word of God (1 Cor 2:13–16).

This wisdom of the cross reflects the true nature of the One who created the heavens and the earth. The reason that the world cannot understand this wisdom is that God must finally reveal its truth. C. S. Lewis captures this mystery in his book *The Lion, the Witch and the Wardrobe*. In the book, Edmund betrays his brother and sisters, the people of Narnia, and even Aslan, the true king of Narnia. He deserves to die—and the White Witch demands that he do so. Aslan strikes a bargain with the White Witch to substitute himself for Edmund. The Witch accepts, and Aslan is sacrificed only to be resurrected. When Lucy and Susan cannot understand what has happened, Aslan replies:

> "It means," said Aslan, "that though the Witch knew the Deep Magic, there is magic deeper still which she did not know. Her knowledge goes back only to the dawn of Time. But, if she could have looked a little further back, into the stillness and darkness before Time dawned, she would have read there a different incantation. She would have known that when a willing victim who had committed no treachery was killed in the traitor's stead, the Table would crack and Death itself would start working backward."[6]

The wisdom of the cross is the Deeper Magic of which Lewis wrote. The cross of Christ reveals the deepest wisdom that underlies and supports all human attempts to live and order our lives. On the cross,

---

6. Lewis, *Lion, the Witch and the Wardrobe*, 74.

the limitations of a human notion of justice is demonstrated and a deeper wisdom, what we might call a "wisdom of grace," is revealed. This wisdom is present in life and death, in success and failure, in deserved blessing and undeserved suffering, in times of radiant meaning and purpose in the dark times when meaning and purpose seem absent.

The Way of Wisdom and New Testament Faith

In our contemporary world people sometimes think of "faith" and "knowledge," and "theory" and "practice," as different categories. We often think of "faith" as a kind of incomplete knowledge, or worse, something people choose to believe in the face of contrary facts.[7] Critics of Christianity often describe faith as irrational—a kind of flight from reason. For these people, "faith" means holding to a belief despite the absence of evidence, or worse, against clear evidence. Even Christians can fall into thinking that faith is something alien to reason, or in some ways, opposed to reason. Much harmful debate between science and religion stems from this way of thinking. In contemporary religious discussion, this opposition of faith and knowledge is often used to radically distinguish the life of faith from the practical life. Gradually, this has resulted in the widespread idea that "faith" is something opposed to "knowledge" or "wisdom."

The false dichotomy between faith and reason is foreign to the spirit of the writers of the Christian Bible and of the early church. For early Christians, the revelation of Christ was a moment of deepened understanding of God and the universe God created. The early church saw the incarnation as a physical revelation—a personal revealing inside of creation of the invisible wisdom of God (Col 1:15–17). This same divine wisdom was also revealed in nature (Rom 1:20). For these writers, practical wisdom, understanding reality and moral

7. This section contains ideas first presented in my book *Centered Living/ Centered Leading*, from which the argument is taken.

knowledge all came from the same source—the uncreated wisdom of God.

For those who accept this ancient Way of Wisdom, scientific understanding, faith, and moral insight are parts of an interconnected web of created rationality binding the physical, moral, and intellectual universe together. Eugene Peterson captures this notion in his paraphrase when he says, "God's law is not something alien, imposed on us from without, but woven into the very fabric of our creation. There is something deep within . . . that echoes God's yes and no, right and wrong" (Rom 2:14 Message). The wisdom of the cross, the wisdom revealed in wisdom literature, and the wisdom revealed by modern science are not opposed to one another. They complete and illuminate one another.

For early Christians, the revelation embodied in Jesus was not a flight into the irrational or into a subjective world of metaphor. Instead, Christ provided a revelatory insight into the deepest rationality of the world. This is why an early Christian could say:

> He is the image of the invisible God, the firstborn of all creation; for in him all things in heaven and on earth were created, things visible and invisible, whether thrones or dominions or rulers or powers—all things have been created through him and for him. He himself is before all things, and in him all things hold together." (Col 1:15–17 NRSV)

For the writer of Colossians and for early Christians generally, the revelation of Christ was a revelation of the ultimate rationality of the universe, the principle of reconciliation between the physical, spiritual, and moral universes. On the cross, God revealed the ultimate nature of deity. In so doing, he established God as self-giving love—a love that is present in the meaninglessness parts of life and in the undeserved suffering we sometimes endure. In the resurrection of Jesus, God was revealing at the very boundaries of human reason the ultimate ground for our hope.

A Life Reordered by Transformational Insight

James Loder speaks of the importance of transformational know-ing—a kind of knowing that re-orders all that we have previously known into a new order—an order that explains what was previously inexplicable and makes rational what was previously irrational.[8] Transformational knowledge comes about as a result of a conviction-al insight that transforms understanding and reorders the human psyche.[9] The revelation of Christ is such a transformational insight. By faith, new understanding is created. This new understanding is not irrational. It is deeper than human rationality. It is not a form of foolishness. It is a wisdom that renders lesser insights foolish. This is the wisdom to which the New Testament writers bore witness.

The Old Testament wisdom writers were on a search for truth—for a true way to find happiness and fulfillment. They did so in the context of their faith and of the revelation of God to Israel. Their quest was confronted with difficulties—difficulties with which they wrestled and sought to resolve. They sensed a deep conflict between the fundamental premises of the wisdom tradition and reality as they knew and experienced it. They saw much undeserved suffering in the world, and the wise life did not guarantee happiness, fulfillment, or meaning. Over long centuries, wisdom writers struggled with these problems as they related to their understanding of God, of wisdom, of morals, and of the rationality of the world. Then, in the life, death, and resurrection of Jesus of Nazareth the disciples experienced a complete reorienting of their ideas about God, about the Law, and about the Prophets.

The revelation they received made sense of what had previously been difficult, if not impossible, to understand, but that revelation required a rethinking of the entire history of Israel, so surprising and revolutionary was its impact. In the figure of Christ, they saw revealed a wisdom of One greater than Solomon (Matt 12:42) and a

8. See Loder, *Transforming Moment*, 93–122, 221–29.
9. Ibid., 33.

prophet greater than Moses (Heb 3:3). In Christ, they saw revealed the character of One who fulfilled the Law and Prophets (Matt 5:17). In the crucified and risen Messiah, they received the clue to a mystery their tradition had so long pondered. They saw revealed a God that was with them in their sin and suffering and was at work in redeeming them and restoring creation in the midst of sin and suffering. In the one life of Jesus of Nazareth, they saw the wisdom of God revealed in the most unexpected yet undeniable way. It was for them—and for us—to work out the implications of that revelation.[10]

Because of the personal nature of the revelation of Christ, no purely mental, cognitive response can ever be sufficient. The proper response of faith is to not simply cognitively accept what God has done in Christ. The word for faith connotes more than acceptance. It also connotes trust, and trust requires an act of personal commitment and will. To trust in Christ and to receive his wisdom is to be converted in our minds (what we think), in our bodies (what we do), and in our hearts (what we feel and will to do). A personal revelation demands a personal response of the whole human person. Wisdom is never a matter of abstract cognitive knowing. Wisdom is practical. It is a matter of knowing and doing in a concrete human life formed in relationship with God, with a concrete community, and with the world.

10. In this section, I use Loder's notion of "convictional knowing" and its stages of conflict, scanning, revelation (what he calls "imagination"), release, and interpretation to express the way in which the revelation of Christ impacted the disciples' (and our) expectation of the Messiah. See Loder, *Transforming Moment*, 35–44.

Questions for Reflection

1. How is it helpful for you to think of the revelation of Christ as giving an answer to the questions raised by Old Testament literature?

2. How do you sense that in Jesus a deeper wisdom than that possible by unaided human wisdom is present to you and to your loved ones?

3. In what ways does Paul's explication of the mystery of the revelation of the self-giving love of God on the cross (1 Cor 1:18–25) help make sense of your own daily life and struggles?

4. Why is it important that our faith in Christ and the wisdom of Christ change not only how we think but also how we act and behave? Does this help you understand James's comment that "Faith without works is dead" (Jas 2:17)?

Then the angel showed me the river of the water of life, as clear as crystal, flowing from the throne of God and of the Lamb down the middle of the great street of the city. On each side of the river stood the tree of life, bearing twelve crops of fruit, yielding its fruit every month. And the leaves of the tree are for the healing of the nations. No longer will there be any curse. The throne of God and of the Lamb will be in the city, and his servants will serve him. They will see his face, and his name will be on their foreheads. There will be no more night. They will not need the light of a lamp or the light of the sun, for the Lord God will give them light. And they will reign for ever and ever.

REVELATION 22:1–5

16

Epilogue: Wisdom and Our Time

We have traveled a long way in this critical-realistic, relational look at wisdom literature. With any luck, the reader senses the opportunity a wisdom approach to the problems of contemporary life offers for a recovery of orderly and successful living in the postmodern world—and a sense of the limits of purely worldly wisdom. Ultimately, proof of the viability of this approach will not be found within these pages. Any real proof must be in lives formed and transformed in a vital, wise, loving relationship with God and others.

Christians in Early Twenty-First Century America

Alisdair MacIntyre begins his book *After Virtue* with a story. "Imagine," he says, "that the natural sciences were to suffer the effects of a catastrophe."[1] He goes on to describe an environmental disaster unfairly blamed on the scientific community. After riots, acts of violence, deaths, and destruction, a "know nothing" party takes control and abolishes the teaching of science in schools and universities. Remaining scientists are imprisoned. After a period of time, there is a change in public mood, and a few leaders attempt to restore and revive the scientific community, though hardly anyone remembers

1. MacIntyre, *After Virtue*, 1.

exactly how science was actually practiced. All that remains are fragments of the great achievements of the past.

Slowly but surely, the group attempts to restore science as a discipline, but it is very difficult. There are no real scientists remaining to lead the effort. There are no remaining university departments of physics, chemistry, biology, and the like. There are only fragments of the body of past scientific literature remaining. Although some of the theorems of science remain known to scholars, they are disconnected and incomplete. Therefore, they memorize parts of the remaining literature, engage in debates over the meanings of certain theories, and attempt to teach children elementary principles of science. Unfortunately, what they are doing does not in any way resemble science.

Then MacIntyre makes his point: moral thinking in the late twentieth and early twenty-first century is in just such a condition. From the beginnings of moral inquiry until the Enlightenment, a form of life dominated Western Europe and a great body of literature developed illuminating and analyzing a way of life formed by the Christian story. Over the past three hundred years, the foundations of Western civilization and culture have been eroded in a period of growing skepticism. We now live among the intellectual and moral ruins of that culture. Worse, all attempts of a purely secular society to create a new foundation for culture have failed spectacularly.

What is sometimes called the Judeo-Christian culture forms the historic foundation of Western life and thinking, but the reality of this culture is far more subtle and complex than its name implies. Both Jews and Christians were profoundly impacted by various cultures of the ancient world and most importantly by that culture we sometimes refer to as "Greco-Roman," the cultures of ancient Greece and Rome. We have already seen that the writers of wisdom literature were deeply impacted by the broader culture of the ancient Middle East, especially Egypt. They in turn were impacted by other cultures with which they came into contact.

By the beginning of the Modern Age (circa AD 1492), medieval culture was in contact with, and impacted by, Muslim culture. In fact a portion of what we call Greco-Roman literature was mediated to the West by Islamic sources. Modern culture has been deeply impacted by the culture of the Far East. All of this impacted the development of Western culture in profound ways. The world created by the Judeo-Christian tradition was far from the creation of "dead white men." It was a rich, deep synthesis of the insights of many cultures over all of human history.

Over the past three hundred years that way of life has been attacked, questioned, ridiculed, distorted, forgotten, diminished, and shattered. All we possess today are fragments. We continue to use expressions from the past, but we no longer have a practical comprehension of much of this long history, so that we have largely lost the actual practices to which the theories referred. The way of life formed by our history has slowly disintegrated. This is true in secular culture. Worse, it is also true among Christians. We use the language of faith, but too often we think, will, choose, and live on the basis of the secular world around us.

A pastor sits alone in his office, near the end of a long winter day. He just finished a counseling session with a young couple. The couple grew up and met years before in church. He married young—and that marriage did not last. It is her first marriage. They have been living together for some time. The pastor reminisces that he rarely marries couples any more who have not lived together before marriage. In addition, there are some red flags that emerged during their time together. The couple renewed their friendship before the end of his marriage. He has a child from his prior marriage. She is not sure about raising someone else's child. She has debts resulting from poor spending habits. Neither has any savings at all. He does not have a regular job, certainly not the kind of job that this pastor would hope for the spouse of one of his children. The world in which he ministers is a far cry from the world of the small Midwestern town where he was raised. "What kind of world do we live in," he thinks, "that young people can stray so far from simple morality and common sense?"

Nowhere is the problem of a loss of cultural heritage more apparent than in the church. Often church members and leaders use traditional language of Christian faith, life, and morality, but that language no longer connects with and forms the concrete reality of their day-to-day lives. Their lives and ours are formed by the values and lifestyle of a culture increasingly irrational and alienated from its history and its roots in the Greco-Roman and Judeo-Christian past. For example, most Christians understand that one of the Ten Commandments prohibits adultery and that marriage is in some sense sacred. Pastors preach sermons on the subject. Members attend Bible studies where the principles are espoused. Guest speakers and cultural commentators speak and write about family values. Christians often send their children to Christian schools where traditional ethics are taught, sometimes too forcefully. Nevertheless, studies show that American Christians often have affairs, divorce, and dishonor marriage in pretty much the same way as non-Christians.

Many young people are frankly nonchalant about the biblical teaching concerning pre-marital sex. As a pastor I can testify to what young people will say and admit to in a safe environment. Publically, many Christian young people mouth the principles of traditional morals—especially in front of their parents and religious leaders. Privately, they find their way around them or ignore them altogether. They do this because the moral world they truly inhabit is formed by the cultural world in which they live and breathe every moment of every day they are not in church or in a Bible study. While they know the language of Judeo-Christian culture, they no longer inhabit and live out the reality of it.

Sex is not the only area in which Judeo-Christian culture no longer meaningfully impacts social behavior. Pre-modern societies normally regulated, and perhaps even overregulated, economic life. There was an attempt to regulate economic life so that the rich and poor could live together without one party taking undue advantage of the other. For example, the limitation of interest rates through usury laws was based upon religious and moral concerns. Now, late modern and postmodern societies, capitalist and socialist, have tended to exclude religious and moral considerations from business and economic policies. The result is that the many Christians and Jews employ strategies in their business lives that the Bible and their respective traditions expressly or implicitly condemn.

There is something deeply misguided in the way in which modern and postmodern people fail to internalize Scripture, the truths of the Christian faith, and the way of life they imply. Even when Christians memorize the foundational texts of the Christian tradition, they often have ceased to express and control the realities of everyday life. On the theological left, the words of Scripture do not have objective content; they merely express religious feelings. On the theological right, the words of Scripture express a proclaimed inerrant content, an infallible truth that is often mentally accepted, but does not impact behavior. In neither case does it seem that these words end up "written on the tablet of the heart" (Prov 3:3).

From Enlightenment to Modernity

What went wrong? The story MacIntyre tells is a hidden retelling of the story of the modern world. There was a time when what might be called Judeo-Christian faith and ethical practices and theories stemming from the works of Plato, Aristotle, St. Augustine, and Thomas Aquinas dominated Western life. The majority of people were Christian, at least in name. The Roman Catholic Church, the monastic orders, and the teachers of the nascent universities in Europe were dominated by the thinking of these great teachers. Yes, there were doubters. Yes, there were other traditions. But the Christian faith and the ethics of Aristotle as modified by Thomas Aquinas reflected an intellectual and moral consensus.

During the Renaissance (1500–1600) and Reformation (1517–1648), this societal consensus began to deteriorate. The Renaissance was a time of rediscovery of the classical Greek tradition. It also was a time when foundations were laid for the convulsions of the Reformation. The Reformation was a time of biblical renewal in faith and morals, but it was also the beginning of the modern questioning of authority, secular and religious. Then, in the 1700s, the Enlightenment began. The Enlightenment was a time when Western Europe discovered the power of human critical reason (Descartes), the method of science (Newton), skepticism towards authority (the French "Philophes"), and belief in human progress (the scientific and industrial revolution).

A central feature of the Enlightenment and the Modern Age has been a rejection of tradition, of religious institutions (especially the Roman Catholic Church), and of any kind of knowledge that cannot be "proved" by human critical reason. The result has been a loss of the social and religious foundations for moral and ethical reasoning. Although our society is a scientific and technical marvel, it is culturally, intellectually, ethically, morally, and spiritually impoverished—with all the human suffering and damaged lives that the word "poverty" implies.

From Modernity to Postmodernity

"What does this have to do with me?" some may ask. The answer is simple: the world in which we live was created, for better and for worse, by the upheaval of the Enlightenment. We see around us the wonders of technology and the results of the scientific method. All of us experience the benefits of modern medicine. All of us understand the benefits of industrialization with the dramatic increasing standards of living. The benefits and progress of the Modern Age have been enormous.

Just as we all experience the benefits of the Modern Age, we also experience its limitations. With the successes of the scientific method, people began to see that method as applicable to all of knowledge—and forms of knowledge, such as religious and moral beliefs, that are not susceptible to scientific proof were often ignored or scorned. With the successes of science and technology, people began to believe that all the problems of human society could be solved by science and its application to human problems.

With the advance of the material aspects of human society, people began to believe that material progress, often visualized in scientific and industrial terms, was both inevitable and potentially unending. Science and human reasoning when applied to the problems of human life and existence would continue to improve human life and provide a final consummation of the yearning of the human heart for meaning, purpose, health, prosperity, goodness, truth, and beauty.

The Postmodern World

Then the tumults of the twentieth century came. Two Great Wars, one ending with the use of a weapon that made possible the destruction of civilization, cast doubt upon the inevitability of progress. The complete destruction of human civilization became as realistic an alternative as its continued progress. The myth of progress and the hope of a human paradise created by science and human reason began to die. A deep moral and spiritual cynicism began to grow until it came to dominate not just elite thinking, but popular culture as well.

Although scientific innovation continued at an accelerated pace and the standard of living continued improving in Western Europe and America, human nature remained the same. Although industrial society continued to develop, socio-economic inequities and environmental degradation began to trouble many people. Amidst the wealth of the West, doubts and anxiety plagued many, many people as the culture lost its historic faith, form of life, and basic morals. In the midst of the successes of Western culture, many people are alienated and doubt that Western faith and ideals will produce a stable future. Increasingly indebted societies reflect an unwillingness to sacrifice for a future in which they no longer believe. Much was gained as a result of the Enlightenment and in the Modern Age, but much has been lost.

Until recently, the moral and practical skepticism and nihilism of intellectual and cultural elites that emerged during the modern period impacted only a small number of people. The majority of people were formed by the moral tradition of the West. But with the increasing importance of the media, the values and beliefs of the few have become the values of the many. We now live in a society without any consistent and widely accepted norm of personal morality and behavior. The results of this phenomenon can be found in every city, town, village, church, school, and neighborhood in America.

Most observers believe that the human race is entering a period that, for now, takes the name "postmodern." In a way, the name reflects an uncertainty concerning the positive aspects of our new cultural environment. All the term "postmodernism" connotes is that the postmodern world emerged "after" the modern world. The content of this civilization is still emerging. We can't see what the postmodern world is or will be like in the future; we only know that the modern era is over. What is to come is unclear.

The pillars of the Enlightenment were confidence in human critical and scientific reason, a faith that human reason, and especially the scientific method, would usher in a kind of Golden Age in which many of the world's most vexing problems were once and forever solved, a belief in a universal morality discernible by reason alone, and hostility towards tradition, traditional forms of life, and traditional religion. Each of these pillars of Enlightenment thinking crumbled under the pressure of the wars and violence of the twentieth century, the terrible suffering inflicted by the ideological regimes of Nazism and Communism, and the perception that Western Capitalism is itself a kind of ideology that has destructive impacts on the environment and on local cultures. Philosophically, the critical posture of philosophers from Nietzsche to the present, and especially the advocates of what is sometimes called "deconstructionism" further undermined a belief in universal reason and morality. Culturally, the growth of education and the rise of what is sometimes called "multiculturalism" further relativized almost any imaginable moral or religious system or belief.[2]

Back to the question, "What does this have to do with me?" Although few of us ponder the deep religious and philosophical issues raised by modern culture, we live in the boiling social and cultural cauldron of its results. Many of our grandparents and great-grandparents grew up in rural communities. Our parents and grandparents built great industries and the cities their growth required. Today, all over the world, many people live in giant metropolises. Most of us live in relatively large cities. Some of us live in great conglomerations of cities, of which the New York-Washington, the Houston-Dallas-San Antonio, and the San Francisco-Los Angeles-San Diego corridors are examples.

Most of us do not live near relatives, parents, aunts, uncles, and grandparents in close-knit extended families. If we listen to or watch the media, we see played out lifestyles deeply at odds with not only traditional Judeo-Christian lifestyles but also deeply at odds with the cultural traditions of Islam, Hinduism, Buddhism, or almost any other traditional cultural norm. Day after day, the popular media, driven by advertising, promotes a culture that is deeply materialistic, deeply romantic, deeply sensual, and (despite its claims to reasonableness) deeply unreasonable.

Those who work in social service agencies and in churches and other religious areas see daily the impact of our common culture on

2. For a Christian introduction to postmodernism, see Veith, *Postmodern Times.*

the lives of ordinary people. Some years ago, my wife and I had the pleasure of doing a pulpit exchange with a pastor in Scotland. (I am a Presbyterian by heritage.) The first day in our new home, a couple came to the manse. They were both Muslim. Their daughter had run away with the son of a pastor in the Church of Scotland.

The family lived in Scotland, far away from the Middle Eastern nation of their ancestors. The father ran a small shop. The mother worked in the shop, where she did not wear traditional garb. The daughter was educated in the public schools and universities of a progressive European nation. Although she professed the faith of her parents, her dress, behavior, and values were those of a typical Scottish young adult. Her parents were traditional Muslims. She was a typical postmodern Briton. Under Muslim law, the girl had forfeited her relationship with her parents, and might even have been beaten or killed. The mother was afraid for her daughter's future. The father was visibly angry. The girl had violated Muslim expectations. The boy had violated one of the oldest teachings of Christian morality—a morality the surrounding culture no longer upholds, and only reluctantly acknowledges forms a part of its heritage. In the end, these two young people were victims of a rootless culture with no real norms or widely held moral and cultural expectations.

For a long time during the Enlightenment and much of the Modern Age, the loss of contact with a tradition of faith and morals did not impact culture in a devastating way. Average people continued to go to church or synagogue. They grew up with their character formed by the saga of Israel and of Christ and the church. They read Plutarch's "Lives of the Noble Romans and Greeks." People knew the old songs and old stories. They lived in a world formed by a heritage that began when God appeared to Abraham and when Socrates walked the streets of Athens. Though intellectual and cultural elites had long ago given up the faith that formed them, their values, morals, and outlook on life were still formed by the heritage they rejected.

With the advent of modern media, and the pervasive impact of movies, television, and the internet, all this has changed. Another story—a story deeply incoherent but filled with seductive images of wealth, power, violence, and pleasure—began to form the character of not just a few but of the many. We now live in the aftermath of that cultural and moral disaster. At best, we live among the fragments of a cultural past. Most of us live among its bombed out ruins, like survivors of the great bombings of the Second World War in Britain, France, Germany, or Japan.

Our life among the ruins of Western civilization breeds root-lessness in many different ways. It is the author's conviction that the deepest need of our culture is to reconnect with the traditional wisdom of the ancient world. This does not mean that we must jettison or reject the accomplishments of the modern world. It does not mean retreating into a pre-modern culture. It means reaching deep beyond and before modernity into the cultural traditions from which the modern world emerged in order to recover the best and most important part of what has been lost. In the West, this involves reaching deep into the Judeo-Christian tradition as well as into the secular roots of our culture found in the cultures of Greece and Rome. Under the cultural conditions of the West today, it also means reaching into the wisdom and moral traditions of other cultures in the quest for wisdom and moral truth.

A New St. Benedict?

Near the end of *After Virtue*, MacIntyre cryptically speaks of the end of Western civilization as we know it and of a "new dark age" in which we now live. This new Dark Age is characterized by a loss of faith in truth and in the reality of spiritual and moral values. Its results are seen in the pervasive spiritual and moral decay of our societies and in the loss of confidence in our institutions. Paradoxically, the Enlightenment, which began with a supreme confidence in human reason, has ended in the creation of a culture that is characterized by a growing irrationality, a loss of faith in the existence of the good, the true, and the beautiful, and a deepening, violent cultural crisis in every society it dominates.

MacIntyre ends *After Virtue* with no answer, only a general direction in which Western culture might go:

> What matters at this stage is the construction of local forms of community within which civility and the intellectual and moral life can be sustained through the new dark ages which are already upon us. And if the tradition of virtues was able to survive the last dark ages, we are not entirely without grounds for hope. This time, however, the barbarians are not waiting beyond the frontiers; they have already been governing us for some time. And, it is our lack of consciousness of this that constitutes part of our predicament. We are waiting not for a Godot, but for another—doubtless very different—St. Benedict.[3]

In this short conclusion McIntyre gives just a clue as to our predicament and to the probable way Western society might find its way out of the new Dark Age.

Benedict of Nursia (493–547), the man we know as St. Benedict, lived at the end of the Roman era, during one of those moments of human history when the world was moving from one cultural milieu to another. The classical world was over. The culture created by Greece and Rome had burned itself out. What we call the Fall of Rome was really the end of a long period of decay as the classical world came to its political, intellectual, moral, and religious end. During Benedict's lifetime Western civilization had already entered a dark time of cultural dissolution and decay.

There are many parallels between Europe at the time of Benedict and our own culture. We also live at a juncture in history. The modern world is over. The world we inhabit is increasingly chaotic. Our culture is experiencing an increase in almost every symptom of cultural decay one can image. At the same time, something different

---

3. MacIntyre, *After Virtue*, 263.

is emerging, a culture we call postmodern, but it is too early to tell precisely what this new culture will be like.

In the midst of the turbulence that surrounded the decline of Rome, St. Benedict created a rule and a form of life that gave order to Catholic monasticism.[4] The achievements of St. Benedict and the other Roman Catholic reformers who created the culture of the Middle Ages were not revolutionary. Indeed they did not intend to be revolutionary. Benedict believed in the truth of orthodox Christian faith and the adequacy of the morality of the Bible and of the Christian tradition. His task, unlike that of the new barbarians among us, was not to create a "new religion," "new morality," or "new society," but to establish the religion, morality, and society of the pre-modern world upon more secure intellectual and practical foundations. Benedict and those who followed him saw themselves not as revolutionaries, but as the inheritors and protectors of a tradition and way of life.

Fundamental to the program of St. Benedict was that the church and society of his day could not be renewed without a visible picture of what a renewed society might look like. The medieval monastic orders were intended to be a kind of embodied picture of what could be—of what the Roman Catholic Church could look like, and what a wise society built on the foundations of Christian faith and practice might look like. The monks lived out their notion of what a renewed Christendom might look like.

The medieval orders were primarily a way of life structured through an institution (the order and monastery) where individuals found meaning and a place in a society in which spiritual values lay at the center of human life. Work, worship, and rest punctuated their days. One can critique the level of success the orders had in achieving their program, but at least they attempted it. For countless people within and without the orders, they were the source of a life

---

4. See Benedict of Nursia, *Rule of St. Benedict*. There are many translations, interpretations, and commentaries on the Rule for those who are interested.

with meaning and purpose devoted to God, to truth, to beauty, and to virtue.

A Life Structured Around Scripture

Benedict, like the Protestant Reformers after him, shaped a way of life structured around the Bible and the story of the Bible. Protestants often critique the Catholic orders as "unbiblical." This prejudice cannot survive a single day living in a community in which all of life is structured around the reading of Scripture and the worship of God. A renewed Western civilization that does not spring from a renewed commitment to a life structured around the biblical story and Christian faith is unlikely to impact our culture in a powerful and lasting way. At the center of any life lived by indwelling the Christian story is the figure of Christ, the Word and Wisdom of God revealed in human flesh for all to see.

Much postmodern criticism has been levied at the foundational texts of Western civilization. In its most infantile form, it is a critique of a civilization created by "dead white men." This, of course, ignores the facts. The "children of Abraham and Sarah" and the writers of the Old Testament were Semites. The "Eastern fathers" were not European and included women as well as men. Augustine was North African. The body of literature they created is culturally diverse in a way that modern thinking often is not. In order to reconstruct a stable and wise Western world in Europe and America, it will be necessary to recover the foundational texts of Western culture as well as add new texts of wisdom as time goes by. It may even be necessary in the face of multiculturalism to reach deep into the wisdom literature of other cultures and incorporate their wisdom into our thinking.[5] Most importantly, any new Benedict/s must recover the Bible and its language in such a way that it becomes written on the heart of contemporary men and women.

5. See my earlier book, *Centered Living/Centered Leading*, which was just such an attempt.

A Life Structured Around Worship

Monastic life was and is structured around worship. The monastic day is structured around the "hours," which include regular worship, not just weekly, but throughout each day. In order for Western civilization to recover a sense of the holy and of human relationship with the Holy, it will have to recover a desire for worship and for a life that finds its structure and meaning in regular cycles of worship involving families, local religious bodies, and even perhaps larger communities of faith.

Secular culture has resulted in a society in which the Sabbath, a day set aside for worship and rest, is a thing of the past, practiced by a few dedicated souls. What used to be "Holy Days" in which families gathered to worship and celebrate the foundations of their faith have become, even for many Christians, days to eat and drink to excess and watch sports. Such a culture soon forgets the sanctity and the holiness of family life.

A Way Recognizing the Moral Nature of Life

Modern culture is rapidly proving the intuition of the ancients that a society without a moral and ethical center must inevitably disintegrate into political, economic, and cultural chaos. Much of our culture is built upon a false exaltation of "individual choice" and a failure to see the reality of personal wisdom and virtue. To say that wisdom, faithfulness, justice, equity, sobriety, and other values are real values is to say that they have existence and potency whether or not any particular individual accepts or recognizes them. It is to say that there is something like a natural law operative in the world—a reality we cannot ignore without consequences.

C. S. Lewis speaks helpfully of this law in his book *Mere Christianity*:

> The Moral Law, or the Law of Human Nature, is not simply a fact about human behavior in the same way the Law of

Gravitation is, or may be, simply a fact about how heavy objects behave. On the other hand, it is not a mere fancy, for we cannot get rid of the idea, and most of the things we say and think about men would be reduced to nonsense if we did. And it is not simply a statement about how we should like men to behave for our own convenience; for the behavior we call bad and unfair is not exactly the same as behavior we find inconvenient, and in fact may even be the opposite. Consequently, this Rule of Right and Wrong, or Law of Human Nature, or whatever you want to call it, must somehow or another be a real thing—a thing that is really there and not made up by ourselves.[6]

Lewis goes on to point out that there is more than one kind of reality. The reality of truth, beauty, and goodness press in on us whether we recognize it or not.[7] The moral universe presses upon us whether we recognize it or not. We cannot safely ignore it without pain to ourselves and the dissolution of our society.

To say that anything is real is to say that it exists independently of our subjective perception and impacts the life and the quality of life of those who come into contact with it. It is in this exact way that wisdom and foolishness operate. Those who cease to see the difference between wisdom and foolishness, between righteousness and wickedness, or between virtuous and dissolute behavior, are unable to make decisions necessary to achieve a happy and whole life. Those who cease to feel that the wisest course of action will be revealed to them by the practice of the virtues are left without the ability to react to the moral nature of the universe which in fact presses upon us all.

A Way of Life Involving Order

The Benedictine renewal involved orders that followed a rule that resulted in a particular way of life. The way of life the members of

6. Lewis, *Mere Christianity*, 28–29.
7. Ibid.

the Benedictine order thought they were recovering was the Way of Jesus as they understood it. It is likely that any recovery of ordered life in the postmodern world will be accompanied by people banding together in order to embody a different way of life than common in our society. In order to do this, they will have to have some structure that defines the way in which they will live out the Way of Christ.

Modern readers of the Benedictine Rule can be put off by the detail it includes concerning the structure of daily life and the relationships among monks. It is helpful to recognize that Benedict was reacting against the disorder of his society and against the mistakes of earlier monastic orders as he created the Rule. His rule both established a way of life and addressed errors found in earlier rules. The success of the Rule is proof of its power and the importance of a kind of pattern with the power to order human life wisely.

The way of wisdom provides an avenue for ordinary people to explore in the conduct of their daily lives to discipline themselves in order to find a better and more satisfying way of life than that urged upon us by the media and by the cultural arbiters of postmodern society. A rediscovery of the value of faith, of tradition, and of traditional ways of ordering life, would result in persons from many parts of the Christian tradition re-thinking and re-ordering their lives in a multitude of ways. A Christian re-discovery of the wisdom tradition would almost certainly cause other traditions to rediscover their own wisdom resources. There may, therefore, be not so much a need for one new St. Benedict as for many. What is certain is that the excessively individualistic and excessively disordered structure of contemporary society does not provide a viable path forward.

Any attempt to provide people with guidance for living will very likely involve looking both at the success of past attempts and overcoming their limitations and mistakes. More than fifteen hundred years have passed since St. Benedict wrote his rule. We can see more clearly than Benedict could see the limitations of the monastic way of life. We can see and understand its successes and failures. In so doing, we can adapt his ideas, and the ideas of others, in crafting a way of following Jesus that is both wise and appropriate to our day and time.

A Way of Life Founded in Family

It has been pointed out that families in the West, and especially families in America, are notoriously weak. One of the Benedictine vows is a vow of stability. A monk is committed to the community for life. A recovery of a wise and healthy culture in the West cannot be accomplished without a renewal of the basic unit of society. Without strengthening and stabilizing family life it is difficult to imagine that there can be a strengthening of community life in the West and especially in America.

Our capacity to live in community is formed in the first community of which we are a part. If wisdom literature is correct concerning the crucial role of the family, then the most basic renewal that is needed is in the life of the family. The new St. Benedicts among us will have to find ways to express a wiser, more stable, and more orderly way of life in the context of concrete human families. Whatever good has come from modern ideas of marriage and divorce, they have ceased to secure for parents or children the kind of stable family life that results in secure and stable adults.

A Way of Life Founded in Community

During one of American's recent political conventions, one person was reported to have said that "our national government is all we have in common." With due respect for our national government and its leaders, this statement expresses a deep problem with our society. Nation states are important; but they are no substitute for families, local communities, and what sociologists call "mediating institutions," such as churches, synagogues, mosques, temples, private associations, and other local institutions. National governments are no substitute for neighborhood associations, townships, cities, and other forms of local community.

It is important that people feel connected to their local community. While no one belongs to all of the possible institutions of local community life, everyone can be happy for the participation of themselves and others in all of them. A renewed Christian way of life will be founded on the deliberate nurture of communities at all levels of society. In order for communities to be nurtured, individuals and churches must be committed to the life of the community so that there can be stable growth and nurture of community life.

A Life Formed in a Rhythm of Labor and Rest

In much of contemporary society, work has supplanted God, family, and community as the center of life. Especially among the successful, work and its accompanying status and benefits has become an idol. In America, success has become the ultimate goal of too many in business, in government, in the media, in academia, in almost all institutions of life.

St. Benedict and his followers created a way of life in which worship, work, community, and rest all find a place. Work is important. In working, human beings fulfill the command to act as stewards of creation and to perfect the world that has been entrusted to our special care and nurture (Gen 1:28). Work is a natural outgrowth of worship, but in overworking, we demonstrate a lack of balance that increasingly warps our full humanity.

What is needed is a recovery of the notion of a rhythm of labor and rest. Sabbath-keeping can be an important part of this recovery, but it is not enough. A day of rest is no substitute for a rhythm of worship, family life, community involvement, work, and relaxation. A renewal of Western culture cannot be accomplished without a renewal of a proper relationship between work and the rest of life.

A Way of Life Founded on Truth

Lesslie Newbigin's book *Truth to Tell: The Gospel as Public Truth* contains a powerful critique of contemporary society and an analysis of its roots similar to the one presented in this chapter. Newbigin speaks about the way in which modern society distinguishes between the public world of scientific facts and the private world of religious and moral truths. Newbigin encourages Christians to have the confidence to proclaim the gospel not just as a truth among many truths, but as The Truth—a truth embodied in the life, death, and resurrection of Jesus Christ. He writes:

> But when the Church affirms the gospel as public truth it is challenging the whole of society to wake out of the nightmare of subjectivism and relativism, to escape from the captivity of the self turned in upon itself, and to accept the calling which is addressed to every human being to seek, acknowledge, and proclaim the truth. For we are that part of God's creation which he has equipped with the power to know the truth and to speak to praise of the whole creation in response to the truthfulness of the Creator.[8]

In the end, any notion of wisdom requires a notion of truth. In order to embody in our lives the spiritual and moral order of the universe in times of trouble, we must believe in its reality. Otherwise we will not develop the humility and dedication needed to seek to understand that moral and spiritual order and adjust our lives to its demands. Human beings will not take any path with confidence and personal commitment, even the path of life, unless they believe that it will actually take us to the place we desire to go—to the wise, happy, and fulfilled life.

The postmodern critique of Enlightenment thinking often reduces all claims to truth to "bids for power," as if every proclamation of truth was simply an attempt to subjugate others. This critique is sometimes levied against the church and against Christian faith.

8. Newbigin, *Truth to Tell*, 13.

The critique may be valid as to some past actions of the church and Christians, but it cannot be levied against the Christian faith in its essence. The Way and Truth that Christians proclaim is the way of the One who came to serve and not be served and who rejected worldly power as a temptation (Matt 20:28; Mark 10:45). For Christians, a renewal of our culture requires a willingness to serve a culture that is often dismissive of our values and hostile to the lifestyles we practice. The days are long gone when we might achieve cultural change by some act of a nonexistent "moral majority." What is now needed is the hard work and diligent ministry of a wise minority. A renewal of wisdom cannot be legislated; it can only be encouraged.[9]

A Way of Life Founded on Love

In the end, the notion of truth that we are called to embody, transmit, and defend is a truth that our society will find almost impossible to understand—it is a truth that can only be known in a community of self-giving love formed in the image of the One who was Truth lifted up on a Roman cross for all the world to see—in the form of a first-century rabbi. It is a truth found in a single person and in an indissoluble unity with self-giving love. It is this personal Truth that desires to be in relation with every human being that we proclaim.

The modern world was dominated by a search for a kind of truth entirely abstracted from human relationships. This quest has ended in the extreme individualism and skepticism of postmodernism. Christian faith proclaims a different sort of truth, a truth that can finally only be expressed in love, a kind of love reflected most clearly on the cross of Christ. This is a truth that cannot be known outside of a *relationship*. It cannot be known abstractly; it must be

9. Perhaps the fundamental mistake of the movements of the 1960s, left and right, was the notion that true cultural transformation for the better can be accomplished through legislation and the power of the nation state. This was an especially mistaken approach for Christians. The One who resisted the temptation to rule the kingdoms of this world and who chose instead to die on a cross works primarily not in overt power but in self-giving service to the world.

beheld and experienced by faith. Christians believe that the search for religious and moral truth cannot be abstracted from the experience of a relationship with the ground of all relationships, the God who is Love. It is in relationship with the God of Love and in a self-giving relationship with our neighbor that we can finally know what cannot be known and find the meaning and purpose in life that we cannot find in the solitude of our own isolated existence.

The communities that rebuild our civilization from the ashes of its current Dark Age will be communities that are built on the character of the One who came not to be served, but to serve, not to be loved, but to love, not to possess, but to be the source of the greatest of all possessions, not to accumulate wealth, but to be the giver of a wealth beyond any human "pearl of great price," not to be wise among the wise, but to be a teacher of a wisdom beyond the wisdom of the wise.

Questions for Reflection

1. Is Alister MacIntyre's parable of a culture that has forgotten the meaning of science helpful to you in understanding what has happened to wisdom and morality in our day and time? Why or why not?

2. If you were to describe in your own words the basic difference between the modern and the postmodern world, how would you describe it?

3. In your opinion, what needs to change in our society to allow children, families, communities, and our culture to flourish?

4. Does the conclusion of the book help you understand what practices and virtues you need to develop, what form of life you need to have to help our culture recover?

Glossary

Convictional Knowing: Convictional knowing is a kind of knowing that impacts understanding of ourselves and the world at the deepest level of the human psyche. Such knowing is achieved by a convictional insight which arises after a problem is recognized, possible solutions are evaluated, insight is achieved and tested, and the insight becomes incorporated into our understanding of the world.

Deep Light: The Apostle John teaches that "God is light," when he says, "This is the message we have heard from him and declare to you: God is light; in him there is no darkness at all" (1 John 1:5). This Divine Light is the divine ground of reason that existed before the created order. It is the "Logos," or Divine Reason immanent in the cosmos. In God, Divine Love and Divine Wisdom exist in harmony, so that love is not separated from wisdom. God's rationality never fails to act in love.

Deep Love: In First John, the apostle also teaches that, "God is love." John says, "Whoever does not love does not know God, because God is love" (1 John 4:8). John goes on to define the nature of this Deep Love when he says, "This is how we know what love is, Jesus Christ laid down his life for us" (1 John 3:16). Jesus says, "Greater love has no one than this, that he lay down his life for his friends" (John 15:13). The Divine Love, Deep Love of God, is a sacrificial, suffering love that loves for the restoration, redemption, and renewal of the Beloved. Jesus Christ revealed this love most clearly on the cross.

Discipline: Discipline has two related meanings in wisdom thought. First, it involves the ability of a person to conform action to wise insight. It is the self-control born of experience and practice. Secondly, discipline refers to the process by which an individual gains the virtue of discipline, the process of reproof, admonition, punishment, and practice that produces this most important virtue. The wise person learns to discipline thought, words, and action.

Fear of the Lord: Fear as applied to God is the kind of deep awe, respect, reverence, or piety appropriate to the God of Israel, the Creator of the heavens and the earth, and the one God among all the false gods of the surrounding nations.

Heart: In wisdom literature the heart is the seat of personality where knowledge and understanding meet in the depths of the human person. When wisdom writers urge that their teachings be written on the hearts of young people, they mean that their teachings are internalized at the deepest level of personality where it serves as an unconscious, tacit source of perception and action.

Insight: Insight is the ability to read between the lines or see into the hidden reality and meaning of a person or situation. An insightful person reads people and situations accurately and forms wise opinions about them that can be translated into effective action in life.

Knowledge: Knowledge in wisdom literature is abstract, conceptual understanding combined with an intimate, existential internalization. This kind of knowledge comes from a word that connotes the kind of intimate knowledge that lovers have of one another. See Personal Knowledge below.

Lord: The term "Lord" was used by the Jews in replacement for the unspeakable name of God given to Moses on Mount Sinai. In this book, the unspeakable name of God is sometimes translated as "The One Who Is" or "The One Who Is and Will Be." These terms refer to the quality of God reflected in his name—the One who is the inexhaustible source of all things.

Personal Knowledge: In this works, Michael Polanyi uses the term personal knowledge to refer to that personal commitment to an understanding of reality that a researcher gains in the process of seeking understanding. In Polanyi's view, there is no "disinterested" understanding of reality because all human understanding is personal and implies personal responsibility for the insight and a willingness to defend it publically.

Proverb: Wisdom is often disclosed as a short, pithy wise saying or allegorical story. The beauty of the proverb is that it is easily remembered, and conveys a truth that is complex and subtle in a short, memorable way.

Righteousness: Righteousness in the Old Testament refers to a life lived in conformity with the Torah or the teachings of God. The goal of the disciplined, wise life is to live righteously in conformity with the will of God.

Tacit Knowledge: In his works, Michael Polanyi describes what he calls "tacit knowledge." Tacit knowledge exists where understanding has been internalized to the point that it unconsciously guides the search for understanding and action. When a carpenter uses a hammer, his focus is not on the hammer but upon the nail he or she intends to drive into the wood. In a similar way, human mental concepts unconsciously guide our understanding and actions as we use ideas to interpret reality.

Way of Wisdom: This term appears in many and varied ways in wisdom literature. The root meaning is "path" or a road one walks upon to get from one place to another. The Way of Wisdom can be the Way of Righteousness (obedience to the moral law), the Way of Wisdom (the ability to make good decisions in life), or the Way of Life (a way that promotes life). In the New Testament, the early Christians are referred to as "people of the Way," which means those who live according to the Way of Christ, whom Christians believe to be the incarnation of the Wisdom or Word of God (see Acts 9:2; 22:4).

Wisdom: Wisdom is the capacity to respond to the challenges of life in an appropriate and successful way. It comes from a root word that connotes the kind of cleverness that is demonstrated in a Middle Eastern bazaar or in business generally. It might be translated as "street smarts," or common sense, or shrewdness.

Bibliography

Aiken, Kenneth T. *Proverbs*. Daily Bible Study Series. Philadelphia, PA: Westminster, 1986.

Arnot, William. *Studies in Proverbs: Laws from Heaven for Life on Earth*. Grand Rapids: Kregal, 1978.

Athanasius. "Four Discourses Against the Arians." In *Nicene and Post-Nicene Fathers*, edited by Philip Schaff and Henry Wace, 303–447. 2nd series, vol. 4. Peabody, MA: Hendrickson, 1994.

Bellah, Robert, et al. *Habits of the Heart*. Berkeley: University of California Press, 1986.

Benedict of Nursia. *The Rule of St. Benedict*. Translated by Anthony C. Meisel and M. L. del Mastro. New York: Image Books, 1975.

Bennett, William J. *The Book of Virtues: A Treasury of Great Moral Stories*. New York: Simon & Schuster, 1993.

Berlin, Adele, and Maxine Grossman, eds. "Money Lending." In *The Oxford Dictionary of the Jewish Religion*, 509. Oxford: Oxford University Press, 1997.

Blenkinsopp, Joseph. *Wisdom and Law in the Old Testament: The Ordering of Life in Israel and in Early Judaism*. Rev. ed. Oxford: Oxford University Press, 1995.

Bonnie and Clyde. Screenplay by David Newman and Robert Benton. Directed by Arthur Penn. Produced by Warren Beatty. Featuring Warren Beatty and Faye Dunaway. Hollywood: Warner Brothers. 1967.

Brunner, Emile. *The Christian Doctrine of God*. Philadelphia, PA: Westminster, 1949.

———. *Dogmatics. Volume 1: The Christian Doctrine of God*. Philadelphia, PA: Westminster, 1949.

Budziszeweski, J. *Written on the Heart: The Case for Natural Law*. Downers Grove, IL: InterVarsity, 1997.

Calvin, John. *Institutes of the Christian Religion*. Edited by John McNeill. Translated by Ford Lewis Battles. Vol. 1. Philadelphia, PA: Westminster, 1960.

Clements, R. E. *Wisdom in Theology*. Grand Rapids: Eerdmans, 1992.

Clifford, Richard J. *The Wisdom Literature*. Nashville, TN: Abingdon, 1998.

Clinton, Hillary Rodham. *It Takes a Village*. New York: Simon & Schuster, 1996.

Come Live with Me. Screenplay by Patterson McNutt. Original story by Virginia Van Upp. Directed and produced by Clarence Brown. Featuring James Steward and Hedy Lamarr. Hollywood: MGM, 1941.

Curtis, Edward M., and John Brugaletta. *Discovering the Way of Wisdom: Spirituality in Wisdom Literature*. Grand Rapids: Kregel, 2004.

Gowan, Donald E. *Bridge Between the Testaments: A Reappraisal of Judaism from the Exile to the Birth of Christianity*. Pittsburgh, PA: Pickwick, 1976.

Guyton, Colin E. *The Promise of Trinitarian Theology*. London: T. & T. Clark, 1991.

Hauerwas, Stanley, and L. Gregory Jones. *Why Narrative? Readings in Narrative Theology*. Grand Rapids, MI: Eerdman's, 1989.

Kennedy, John F. *Profiles in Courage*. Foreword by Robert F. Kennedy. New York: Harper & Row, 1964. Reprinted with new introduction by Caroline Kennedy. New York: HarperCollins, 2003.

Kittel, Gerhard, and Gerhard Friedrich. "Arête." In *Theological Dictionary of the New Testament*, 77–78.

———. "Logos." In *Theological Dictionary of the New Testament*, 505–14.

———. *Theological Dictionary of the New Testament*. Edited and translated by Geoffrey Bromiley. Abridged ed. Grand Rapids: Eerdmans, 1985.

Kung Fu. Television series. Created by David Spielman. Directed and produced by Jerry Thorpe. Developed, written, and co-produced by Herman Miller. Featuring David Carradine, John Carradine, Keith Carradine, and Keye Luke. New York: ABC, 1972–1975.

Lewis, C. S. *The Abolition of Man*. New York: Collier, 1947.

———. *The Lion, the Witch and the Wardrobe*. New York: HarperCollins, 1978.

———. "Men without Chests." In *The Abolition of Man*, 11–35. New York: Collier, 1947.

———. *Mere Christianity*. London: Collins Fontana, 1952.

Loder, James E. *The Transforming Moment*. 2nd ed. Colorado Springs: Helmers and Howard, 1989.

MacIntyre, Alistair. *After Virtue*. 2nd ed. Notre Dame, IN: University of Notre Dame Press, 1984.

Morgan, Don F. *The Making of Sages: Biblical Wisdom and Contemporary Culture*. Harrisburg, PA: Trinity Press, 2002.

Newbigin, Lesslie. *Foolishness to the Greeks: The Gospel and Western Culture*. Grand Rapids: Eerdmans, 1986.

———. *The Gospel in a Pluralist Society*. Grand Rapids: Eerdmans, 1989.

———. *Truth to Tell: The Gospel as Public Truth*. Grand Rapids: Eerdmans, 1991.

Nicene Creed. In *Book of Confessions*, 1–3. Louisville, KY: Presbyterian Church, 1999.

Perdue, Leo G., et al. *Families in Ancient Israel*. Louisville, KY: Westminster John Knox, 1997.

Pierce, C. S. "Review of the Works of George Berkeley—1871." In *Charles S. Pierce: The Essential Writings*, edited by Edward C. Moore, 51–63. New York: Harper & Row, 1972.

Polanyi, Michael. *The Logic of Liberty: Reflections and Rejoinders*. Indianapolis, IN: Liberty Fund, 1951.

———. *Personal Knowledge: Towards a Post-Critical Philosophy*. Chicago: University of Chicago Press, 1958.

———. *Science, Faith and Society*. Chicago: University of Chicago Press, 1946.

———. *The Tacit Dimension*. Gloucester, MA: Peter Smith, 1983.

Polanyi, Michael, and Harry Prosch. *Meaning*. Chicago: University of Chicago Press, 1975.

Polkinghorne, John. *Exploring Reality: The Intertwining of Science and Religion*. London: SPCK, 2005.

———. *Faith of a Physicist*. Princeton, NJ: Princeton University Press, 1994.

———. *The God of Hope and the End of the World*. New Haven, CT: Yale University Press, 2002.

———. *Science and Providence: God's Interaction with the World*. Philadelphia, PA: Templeton Foundation, 1989.

Polkinghorne, John, ed. *The Trinity and an Entangled World: Relationality in Physical Science and Theology*. Grand Rapids: Eerdmans, 2010.

Schwartz, Cindy. "In the End." Sermon on Daniel 7 presented at Advent Presbyterian Church, Memphis, TN, July 24, 1012.

Scruggs, G. Christopher. *Centered Living/Centered Leading: The Way of Light and Love*. Rev. ed. Memphis, TN: Permissio Por Favor/Shiloh, 2010.

———. "Lack of Good Jobs is a Spiritual Issue." *Memphis (TN) Commercial Appeal*. June 2, 2012, M3–M4.

Singer, Michelle. "Letters Reveal Mother Teresa's Secret." *CBS News* (October 9, 2009).

Story, Louise, and Gretchen Morgenson. "S.E.C. Accuses Goldman of Fraud in Housing Deal." *New York Times*, April 16, 2010.

Torrance, Thomas F. *The Ground and Grammar of Theology*. New York: T. & T. Clark, 1980.

———. *Theological Science*. New York: Oxford University Press, 1969.

Toy, C. H. *Proverbs*. International Critical Commentary. Edinburgh, Scotland: T. & T. Clark, 1899, reprint 1979.

Toye, Richard. *Churchill's Empire: The World that Made Him and the World He Made*. New York: Henry Holt, 2010.

Tzu, Lao. *Tao Te Ching: A New English Version*. Translated by Stephen Mitchell. New York: Harper & Row, 1988.

Tzu, Sun. *The Art of War*. Translated by Samuel B. Griffith. Oxford: Oxford University Press, 1963.

Unger, Merrill F., and William White Jr., eds. "Wisdom." In *Nelson's Expository Dictionary of the Old Testament*, 473–76. Nashville, TN: Thomas Nelson, 1980.

Veith, Gene Edward. *Postmodern Times: A Christian Guide to Contemporary Thought and Culture*. Irvine, CA: Crossway, 1994.

von Rad, Gerhard. *Wisdom in Israel*. Valley Forge, PA: Trinity International, 1972.

"The Way of the Tiger, the Sign of the Dragon." In *Kung Fu*, season 1, episode 1. New York: ABC, February 22, 1972.

Westermann, Claus. *Roots of Wisdom: The Oldest Proverbs of Israel and Other People*. Translated by J. Daryl Charles. Louisville, KY: Westminster John Knox, 1995.

Whitehead, A. N. *Adventure of Ideas*. New York: The Free Press, 1933.

Whitehead, Barbara Dafoe, and David Popenoe. "The State of Our Unions: Social Health of Marriage in America 2003." *Theology Matters* 10, no. 2 (March/April 2003) 1–8.

Wild in the Streets. Directed by Barry Shear. Featuring Christopher Jones, Shelly Winters, Hal Holbrook, and Richard Prior. Hollywood: American International Pictures, 1968.

Wittgenstein, Ludwig. *Tractatus Logico-Philosophicus*. London: Kegan Paul, 1922.

Zizioulas, John D. *Being as Communion: Studies in Personhood and the Church*. London: Darton, Longman and Todd, 1985.